The Sea Priest

(Inner voyages to Light)

Alan Richardson

Alan Richardson has been writing weird, winsome and frequently embarrassing books for longer than many of his readers have been alive and is insanely proud of that fact. He has done biographies of such luminaries as Dion Fortune, Aleister Crowley, Christine Hartley, William G. Gray and his own grandfather George M. Richardson M.M. & Bar. Plus novels and novellas that are all set in his local area, along with scripts of same. He has a deep interest in Earth Mysteries, Mythology, Paganism, Celtic lore, Ancient Egypt, jet fighters, army tanks, Wiltshire tea shops, Great British Actors and Newcastle United Football Club. He does not belong to any group or society and does not take pupils because most of the time he hasn't a clue what is going on.

The Sea Priest is another indulgent book self-published via KDP, uploaded to the Creatrix on December 6th 2019, the Moon a waxing crescent.

I don't have a web site, am not on LinkedIn, and I don't do blogs. A more detailed list of my published work can be found somewhere on Amazon Books.

Anyone with a pressing need to contact me can do so via: *alric@blueyonder.co.uk* but please don't attach your manuscripts and ask for 'an honest opinion' because I will always fib.

Some published books

Geordie's War – foreword by Sting
Aleister Crowley and Dion Fortune
The Inner Guide to Egypt *with Billie John*
Priestess - the Life and Magic of Dion Fortune
Magical Gateways
The Magical Kabbalah
The Google Tantra - How I became the first Geordie to raise the Kundalini. *new edition retitled as…*
Sex and Light – how to Google your way to God Hood.
The Old Sod *with Marcus Claridge*
Working with Inner Light *with Jo Clark*
Spirits of the Stones.
Earth God Rising - the Return of the Male Mysteries.
Earth God Risen
Gate of Moon
Dancers to the Gods
Inner Celtia *with David Annwn*
Letters of Light
Me, mySelf and Dion Fortune
Bad Love Days
Short Circuits
The Templar Door
Searching for Sulis
The Quantum Simpleton

Fiction
The Giftie
On Winsley Hill
The Fat Git – the Story of a Merlin
The Great Witch Mum – *illustrated by Caroline Jarosz*
Dark Light – a neo-Templar Time Storm
The Movie Star
Shimmying Hips
du Lac
The Lightbearer
Twisted Light
The Moonchild
The Giftie – in her own words.

Dedication

My wife Margaret
&
My equally loved daughters:

&
Judith Page as ever and always
Mel Knight of Thyme-Raven for her pyrography
Anthony Arundell for finding Kim Seymour
Annie and Frank Blades
John and Janet Maxwell
Tim and Jenny Owen
Fran Simpson and Freddy
Peter and Kath Stokell

The cover has been adapted by me from
www.goodfreephotos.com
I've left the spine and back cover free of words
(I don't know why)

Table of Contents

Modern Kelpies sculpted by Andy Scott in Falkirk

Confession. Explanation. Apology.

In the beginning, I planned to sail this book toward Brittany and track down Morgana le Fay, even peering through her witch-mists to the peculiar heart of Atlantis, where I thought she might be lurking. I was determined to summon, stir and call her up. In the event, at the very start of my literary voyage I was boarded by a very real Celtic Christian named Moluag, and was driven by strange inner currents toward an island in the Hebrides that wouldn't let me go.

The original title of this book was to be *Raasay – an Inner Route to Everywhere*. Somehow, I touched on that island as a living entity rather than just the barren lump of rock and soil, as I had assumed it was. Raasay and Moluag, with the unlikely help of William Wordsworth, have taught me that we can all make voyages that are tied in with the fertile magick of the Earth, its Seas, and our own daily experience. It was written as I went along, never seeing beyond the horizon as to what the next paragraph would reveal. As such it's more a casual journal and an inner travelogue than an attempt at a text-book.

The Sea Priest, I hope, offers help in navigating your own inner voyages. And as Lao-Tzu commented in the sublime *Tao Te Ching*:

> Without going outside, you may know the whole world.
> Without looking through the window, you may see the ways of heaven.
> The farther you go, the less you know.
> Thus the sage knows without travelling;
> He sees without looking;
> He works without doing.

This is as much a set of simple inner techniques that we can all adapt and make use of, as it is about a historical person and geographical destination.

I still haven't been to the island of Raasay itself, although what I have learned of it from afar makes me weep at its beauty, and humbled by the timeless warmth of the community. I feel sure that Moluag (I refuse to call him 'Saint'), has got a lot more to teach me – to teach us all – in future.

And as for Morgana le Fay, well, you might want to read on...

Raasay

Chapter 1

I have never been to Raasay, and despite glimpsing it from afar I will never go. I say that now, right off, in case any readers feel their heart sinking at the thought of yet another impossible pilgrimage being dangled in front of the chakra on their brows. Bear with me as I try to explain my rationale for starting a Quest with a non-journey...

I first saw Raasay from a distance when I had driven over the Pass of the Cattle, the highest road in Britain, in the Highlands of Scotland. I spent the climb trying not to look at the sheer drop on the passenger side, and wrestling with a poor handbrake that was a vital item in all the steep passing places of the narrow but otherwise excellent road. The views at the top, before it descends toward Applecross, had been described to me by many as among the finest in the world.

Crossing the *Bealach na Ba,* to give it the true Gaelic name, is something you don't forget. You are warned, at the very beginning, by a large sign saying that the road is not suitable for learner drivers, caravans and very large vehicles. It is a single track road with some Alpine-like hairpin bends, although if you're a confident and experienced driver these are not too difficult. Fortunately I'm a confident, experienced and irritatingly smug driver so I took the sign as a challenge. The greatest problem was to keep my eyes fixed on the road and not get distracted by the majestic scenery. As it was, the rain at the very top of the pass was so heavy that I never got to see the views out toward the Hebrides that everyone raves about.

We descended to the little village of Applecross and then picked up the coastal road to make a deosil drive around to Plockton. And that was when the skies cleared and I saw Raasay, out to the West – a direction that has ethereal significance in my heart at least. If you know your Tolkien and your elven lore, you'll know what I mean. And if you also know your Egyptian lore you will grasp that all dead souls always head West.

I can't say that Raasay represented either Lothlórien or Amenti. It wasn't bathed in the setting sun or a gibbous moon; It didn't evoke a siren-call from the mystical Celtic islands of Hy-Brasil or Tír Na nÓg. Nor did it ooze with the bleak and compelling atmosphere you get in Skandi thrillers, where landscape and weather are as important as the characters. It was just a long, solid finger of an island in a cold grey sea that stretched 14 miles from north to south, and no more than 3 miles east to west, with waves bashing against its cliffs.

I couldn't say why that island should have fixed itself into my memory other than because I liked the look of its name: *Raasay*. I've only to say it and the image springs up firm and solid as the first, last and only time I saw it. The name is from the Old Norse, meaning Isle of the Roe Deer, or even Island of the Horse. I had no sense that any human could possibly live there now, although apparently some 200 do.

Historically, it's greatest inhabitant seems to have been the little-known Saint Moluag. *Mo* was an honorific, and so his personal name was probably *Lugaid, Luoc or Lua*. He took the road of 'white martyrdom', which was the path of those hermits who adopted a strict asceticism. As a near-contemporary of the mighty Saint Columba, he became active during the period of the First Order of Celtic Saints, and was known as 'The Clear and Brilliant, The Sun of Lismore in Alba'. The First Order were regarded as having been 'most holy: shining like the sun'.

Moving forward some 1400 years, the most recent inhabitant with any claim to fame is the Gaelic poet Sorley MacLean who died in 1996 a the age of 85. He didn't become famous until the 1970s when his very powerful, startling, and multi-level poetry was translated into English. One of his most evocative works, *Hallaig*, begins in translation: 'Time, the deer, is in the wood of Hallaig'. Every Gaelic speaker insists that in the original language every word, every image, has a subtlety that mere English cannot quite express, and I don't doubt that.

Of course I've learned all this in bits and pieces over the years, and have sometimes wondered if some spirit from Raasay was lurking around the edges of my psyche and using the image of the island like a kind of flash-card, to get my attention. But no, that was never the case. I will, one day, look further into the lives and work of both Moluag and MacLean with an historian's intent, but it was the perception of an altogether different poet who helped make sense of why the sight of Raasay has both pleasantly haunted and slightly taunted me for some 13 years now.

Let me digress just a little more...

I was born in 1951. Every school child of my generation (and probably four generations before me) had to learn by heart and/or copy out the poem *Daffodils* by William Wordsworth - sometimes also known by its first line. The first of four verses goes:

> I wandered lonely as a cloud
> That floats on high o'er vales and hills,
> When all at once I saw a crowd,
> A host, of golden daffodils;
> Beside the lake, beneath the trees,
> Fluttering and dancing in the breeze.

He wrote this in 1802 after a long walk around Ullswater in the English Lake District but modified it slightly over the next decade in the face of hostile criticism. Lord Byron took time off from tupping his own sister to comment that he thought the poem puerile, but how many people today can quote a single line of Byron's poetry? Even Wordsworth's best friend Samuel Taylor Coleridge, high on opium as he worked on *Kubla Khan*, thought *Daffodils* was full of 'mental bombast'. Yet the court of public opinion decided wholeheartedly in Wordsworth's favour. A recent British survey of all time favourite poems placed this third, although I personally wouldn't go *that* far.

In comparison with the hard, tough poetry which has emerged in the two centuries since, from the likes of W.B. Yeats, Dylan Thomas, Robert Frost, Sylvia Plath, Ted Hughes, Allen Ginsburg and ten thousand varied others, there is a tendency to think that Wordsworth and all he wrote was somewhat soppy. Yet the man himself was a real Nature Mystic, a pantheist who believed that a divine spirit pervades all the objects of nature. Nature to him was a living being, and if you sought to commune with it, even through such a passive act as observing some distant daffodils, then you can contact something higher than your mortal and mundane self. To him, all is God and God is all.

And – I speak from experience here – the path of the Nature Mystic has its own hard and tough lessons to impart. William, in the heart of the mountains, fells, lakes and silver streams of Cumberland, did not spend his time simpering while he tip-toed through tulips. He knew that when you *really* touch upon the Spirit of Nature you get the whole thing: seasons and cycles, death and darkness, storms and quiet benisons, cold and sunshine and hail and pouring rain and... moments of utter beauty and stillness. In a sense it is the final verse of *Daffodils*, which none of us as schoolchildren ever got as far as remembering, that is the most important:

For oft, when on my couch I lie
In vacant or in pensive mood,
They flash upon that inward eye
Which is the bliss of solitude;
And then my heart with pleasure fills,
And dances with the daffodils.

But all that is something of an apologia that will enable me to introduce
the few lines from a much later poem that helped me make sense of
Raasay. These are from his *Prelude*, that he worked on for most of his life.
In fact he himself never gave it a title beyond the *Poem (title not yet fixed
upon) to Coleridge*. It was a continuous work on the growth of his own
mind and the relevant lines are:

> *There are in our existence spots of time,*
> *That with distinct pre-eminence retain*
> *A renovating virtue, whence, depressed*
> *By false opinion and contentious thought,*
> *Or aught of heavier or more deadly weight,*
> *In trivial occupations, and the round*
> *Of ordinary intercourse, our minds*
> *Are nourished and invisibly repaired;*
> *A virtue, by which pleasure is enhanced,*
> *That penetrates, enables us to mount,*
> *When high, more high, and lifts us up when fallen*[i]

We all have these 'spots of time', as he so deliciously defines them. They
stay there throughout our lives, beyond reason, pure and clear, no matter
what, and retain the 'renovating virtue' that can nourish and repair us. The
spots are often so tiny, so fleeting in their original appearance, that we can
often blink them away like dirt on the eyeball, but they never *quite*
dissolve. They are rarely images of the big things, such as marriage,
divorce, having children. Or of the wordly gains involving house, car,
work, money, travel and the rest. Your life may be in a dark and fierce
phase but by dwelling, even momentarily, on one of these spots in time
and all that they encapsule, then some of the torment can be lifted.

Wordsworth believed that our true learning and education comes
through Nature, and he makes no distinction between caring for the potted
plants within your apartment in the middle of a megalopolis, or hugging a
tree in a remote forest. There is, or should be, an innate sympathy between
our deepest mind and the spirit of Nature, and if you work on that then
you can find harmony. After a visit to Tintern Abbey, which is an

atmospheric and hugely haunted place in the Wye Valley on the border between England and Wales, he wrote in his poem of that name:

> *...And I have felt*
> *A presence that disturbs me with the joy*
> *Of elevated thoughts; a sense sublime*
> *Of something far more deeply infused,*
> *Whose dwelling is the light of the setting suns,*
> *And the round ocean and the living air,*
> *And the blue sky in the mind of man*

To him, if you make no attempt to learn from Nature then your life is worthless, and whatever you might achieve in material terms has no value at all.

Wordsworth, soppy? In that formless tundra that existed behind his eyes and before his mind he walked through lightnings. In his own way, he was as much a warrior as those who try to blast their way inward via robes and rites and incense and oils and crystals and magical weaponry and loudly-shouted Words of Power. I speak from experience here too.

He showed us that we all can explore this inner realm which is also our outer realm, either through something as simple and soppy as glimpsing distantly waving daffodils, or through an active engagement with this all important entity known as Nature.

Which brings me back after divers twists and turns and ramblings to Raasay, which is my own 'spot in time'. Yet I guarantee that every person reading this sentence will, at this very moment, be scanning their memories for moments that might be their own 'spots'.

I can't be dogmatic or precious about how these might float into *your* awareness. For me, Raasay is a singularity. Although I've had a long life with a multitude of exceptional moments both good and bad, none of them have formed themselves into such a solid image as that island. My question, and yours too, must be: If time and space and events are congealing into this Wordsworthian 'spot', what can be gained from it now? William himself experienced a 'renovating virtue' and I can certainly get a sense of that during those unexpected moments when Raasay floats into my psyche. But I think that the island, my 'spot in time', is hinting at more. If we can think of such things as akin to icons on a touch-screen, what might open up if we press them?

This is what I hope to find out with respect to an island I've never visited and never will visit, yet which has pressed on *me* over the years.

Hopefully, by doing so, you will all be able to make sense of your own spots in time.

Chapter 2

October 2ⁿᵈ

I don't know what the tides and currents are like around Raasay, but they must be fierce. Strangely, the tides and currents of my musings about it are rather gentle. As you might guess, I'm learning about the actual island and my 'spot in time' as I go along. No sooner do I create a sentence then I get splashed by a whole lot of 'perhaps', like the waves that fringe the cliffs of Raasay. This is not unpleasant, but nor was it my original intention. I had thought that I'd be done with the island after the first chapter, using it only as a f'r instance. And then I'd segue on to looking at deeper issues involving Morgana le Fay and the Lady of the Lake. Perhaps I'll achieve that by the third chapter, but at the moment Raasay won't let me go. My thoughts are drifting around like a cork on a wave or a message in a bottle. I have no idea where the cork will go or what the message might say. So where should I concentrate my thoughts?

Well, as I drove along the road from Applecross to Plockton that day and caught my first sight of the island I would have seen the flat-topped summit of Dun Caan, the highest hill on Raasay. If I had actually gone there and climbed that summit as James Boswell did during his famous tour of the Highlands and Islands with Samuel Johnson, I too might have danced a jig in delight at astonishing views. On the way up I would have passed by the small Loch na Mna (Lake of the Woman) where legend has it that a tricksy *each-uisge* or water-spirit resides.

The *each-uisge* are shape-sifters that can disguise themselves as a fine horse, pony, a handsome man, seductive woman or even an enormous bird. They are sometimes also known as *Kelpies,* although these tend to be more connected with rivers and streams, though still having the shape of the horse as its primary form. Maybe this is why Raasay has also been called the Island of the Horse? Kelpies trick people into stroking their manes but then drag their helpless victims into the cold depths of their watery homes. Saint Moluag had a lot on his plate, I'm thinking.

It's odd, but now, as I simply muse about peering into that potently named Lake of the Woman, my mind floats very determinedly back to another liminal place and time in my life when a very strong current took a hold and swept me away...

Fifty years ago, when I became obsessed and driven by anything to do with the Western Magical Traditions, those words about Saint Moluag as part of the Celtic First Order, and 'most holy, shining like the sun' would have made me shiver with excitement. I would have felt that a Quest was about to reveal itself. Perhaps it still is! While I have possibly gained a teensy tiny bit of wisdom in the intervening decades, I might also have lost some of the awesome powers of child-like innocence. And I regret that.

Ironically, my first detailed glimpse of those Western Traditions was when I was 18 and visiting the entirely *Eastern* Mystical Traditions of the Samye-Ling Monastery in the Scottish Borders. I was shown around by the very gracious Tibetan abbot Akong Tulku Rinpoche, and tried to impress him with my knowledge of dorjes, chortens, Kangyurs, Red Hat practitioners of Bön-Po and katas.

'Do you speak Tibetan?' asked the abbot, mildly impressed or perhaps just irritated by my teenage style of knowing all things and wandering around like Johnny-Head-in-Air.

I shook my head but didn't try to explain. Quite simply I just read everything I could find about Tibet, and when I was 15 I spent my pocket money of 10 shillings to join the Tibet Society of Great Britain. Then, I wanted nothing more than to go to the monastery of Chakpori and become one of the Lung-Gom-Pa running lamas.

But then my eye was drawn to a solitary book in the little (very little) shop. This was Francis King's *Ritual Magic in England: 1887 to the present day*. I already had a sensationalist, blurry notion of this thing called 'Magic' from the supernatural thrillers of Dennis Wheatley and Algernon Blackwood, plus a few of the technical writings of W.E. Butler and William G. Gray, but I had no real knowledge of history or tradition. Although I couldn't afford to buy King's book there and then, I briefly excused myself from the abbot and dipped inside it. The names and terms leapt out of the pages like spawning salmon returning to their source: First Order, Third Order, Hermetic Orders, Adepts and Sun Masters; the Stella Matutina, Golden Dawn, Amoun Temple, Cromlech Temple; Mathers, Crowley, Yeats, Fortune, Brodie-Innes... It was all so exciting and somehow all so damned familiar. If the book itself was a shape-shifting, seductive kelpie then it could have dragged me down into whatever depths it wanted. I closed and replaced it on its shelf, knowing that as soon as I got back to Newcastle I would beg, borrow or steal to get a copy.

The abbot looked at me.

'Most of the people here are mentally ill,' he said quietly, pointing to several long-haired hippy-types sprawling on couches, glassy-eyed, each one perhaps peering into secret lochs and trying to master the kelpies therein. He made no judgement on them, and neither did I. Perhaps he was

16

just warning me. Perhaps he had glimpsed a path forming before me that would take me far from his Eastern Traditions and so he feared for my own mental health if I took such a route.

He needn't have worried.

But you see, Francis King's tome apart, there was a young side of me that wanted to believe this lama was one of the wonder-workers I had read so much about - and perhaps he was. Many years after that meeting I read how Dr. Arthur Guirdham, lying on a Scottish hillside, had been coaxed out of his body and onto the astral plane by a Tibetan lama. I like to think that this was Akong Tulku Rinpoche. When he said goodbye to me at the Samye-Ling monastery in the south-west of Scotland, he might have seen me heading off ever Westward from then on.

Which somehow, without any rhyme or reason, brings me back to the edges of Loch na Mna on Raasay again.

What I'm experiencing with respect to the island, is that in trying to make sense of this 'spot in time', an awful lot of other images and energies have flown in unexpectedly, like the sea eagles who soar around Beinn Bhàn. I think that I might change the Wordsworthian concept from 'spot' into 'bud'. I think that Raasay for me is a '**bud** in time': a tiny, compact little flower that opens unexpectedly and displays numerous astonishing petals that are aspects of my own inner life. And more importantly, going back to Wordsworth's revelations, because All is One, and One is All, then they are necessarily unfolding aspects of *your* life too.

Intellectually, I really have been trying to break away from the first chapter and get back on track with my original scheme, but something else keeps floating in at more subtle levels. Morgana le Fay, the Lady of the Lake and the nine priestesses on the Isle of Sein will have to wait. Raasay just won't go away.

So the thoughts around Raasay are now, on a rainy Friday night, all lapping against my musings and I can only go with them. Their tides seem to be coming in, rather than out, although they're doing so gently. Goodness knows what flotsam and jetsam they carry.

I think, though, that I'll have to be careful about someone like Saint Moluag. He might well be a tricky, shape-shifting *Each-uisge* wanting me to reach into a magick pool of memory and try to stroke his Celtic, brow-to-brow tonsure. And then I'd just get sucked in.

How serious am I?

To be honest, I'm not sure whether my answer is: *Largely so*, or *Not entirely*.

I'm not talking about a malevolent entity on the inner planes that is masquerading as a Being of Light – at least I don't think I am. If Akong Tulku Rinpoche was right about those damaged souls crashed out on the outer plane of his monastery, then I can tell you that not every being on the *inner* planes is bursting with spiritual goodness - even if they are reckoned to be Saints. Since that time at Samye Ling my life has been devoted to considering what these inner plane Beings are, and what they might want from me. Yet... even as I write that I realise the term 'devoted' is largely wrong. It implies a soppy kind of attachment when really the process was one of benign compulsion. Over numerous driven decades, here is what I've learned...

1500 years ago, people were very different to what we are today. We wouldn't understand a word of their language and would probably be startled by their attitudes. If we could time-travel and see these Celtic Saints like Moluag in person, they would likely seem disturbing and even perhaps mentally ill. They might be icons in the sense of being:

a) images on the computer screen that can open up when touched.

b) icons in the religious sense that have very little substance at all.

But just because they are dead, it doesn't mean they are wiser than we are. Sometimes, when you touch upon these ancient spirits, they are just shells with only a few automated responses to offer, no matter how they might present themselves.

And it's not always clever to think in terms of 'Good' and 'Evil'. Just because Moluag was a Celtic Christian (I'll come back to that later), it doesn't mean that he was a tree-hugging eco-warrior dripping kindness and compassion and equalities in a way that the rotten Roman Catholic Church rarely did.

Mind you, I'm a keen fan of the Celtic Church in Britain and feel that its eventual destruction by the Roman Catholic hierarchies was one of the worst things to happen to the world. In fact the exemplars of the latter were, with rare exceptions, no different to the militant soldiers of ISIL that cause such damage today with their 'convert or die' philosophies.

So I'm inclined to have a natural sympathy for his mission on Raasay and other places. I fancy a quick peek into that Loch na Mna to see if I can catch a glimpse of him or a kelpie. We can access such places via myths and/or self-created pathworkings; we can contact inner beings through mock-ups; but ultimately it is the solid Earth stuff that will not betray us or disappoint. The inner beings have their own agenda. If there's any fragment of consciousness still connected to Moluag then I'll cordially invite him/it into my psyche for the duration of this project, however it turns out.

I'll let you know how we get on.

I'm really not sure why I was initially drawn toward the 'Lake of the Woman'. It's certainly a powerful title and evokes, for me at least, all sorts of links with the Mother, the Great Mother, the Goddess, the amniotic fluid from which we all spring and those timeless, heretical priestess figures that can set our pulses racing. Perhaps I didn't expect to find something of that ilk on the remote emptiness of Raasay. I was about to leave that island behind and press on, when I got an email from my dear pal Judith Page. Judith is a beautiful, awesomely talented artist, uncompromisingly Australian, and one of the Real Ones when it comes to Magick. We've tried several times to co-write books but she is so intellectually ahead of me that we've never quite gelled in that respect. I'm not being falsely modest here. I just can't do scholarly. Or humble.

She knew that I was aiming, in broad terms, to do something about Morgana le Fay, and having lived in Brittany for some time she pointed out the best places to visit. I did, already, have a decent knowledge of that beautiful and eldritch part of the world and had driven all around it when I was in my 20s. I was trying to find traces of a Celtic Saint Ywi, with whom I felt a past-life connection. Then, I saw the tempting signposts to *Val sans Retour* associated with Morgana, and *La Fointaine de L'Eternelle Jeunesse* next to Merlin's Grave yet I was too busy on my own Quest and disappearing up my backside to make even a brief detour. That's another thing I've always regretted. But in her email she mentioned in passing the *Miroir aux Fees* (Faeries' Mirror) which is a large lake  nestled in the deep of the forest, at one end of the Valley of No Return. I'd never heard of *that*!

Of course this made my nape hairs prickle. I'll tell you what I've learned about the Faery Mirror Lake in a moment but the Loch na Mna seems to want a bit more attention first. I'm still not sure why, as I can't imagine that the kelpies, if I can use that term, are wanting to come into my world in the far south-west of the country.

I wrote ten minutes ago that we can access such places via myths, folk-tales and/or self-created pathworkings, so let me tell you the story behind Raasay's magick loch first...

It seems that a blacksmith from Raasay lost his daughter to the each-uisge in the loch. In revenge, he and his son roasted a sheep on the edge of the waters. At last a great mist appeared from the loch and the each-uisge burst out from the waters and seized the offering. Upon which the two men rammed red-hot hooks into the creature's flesh and after a short, brutal struggle, killed it. In the morning after, there was nothing left of the each-uisge apart from a strange, jelly-like substance.

This may be why it is called 'Lake of the Woman', but the authors of the Isle of Raasay website go on to comment:

> The 'jelly-like substance' mentioned is the so-called 'Star jelly', sometimes known as 'astromyxin' or 'Star rot'. Reports of this substance apparently date back hundreds of years but it features heavily in folklore and paranormal tales from the 19th century. This gives an indication of when this particular telling of the story was probably invented.[ii]

I've never heard of 'Star jelly'. Doing a quick google I was pleased to find there is a whole page devoted to it in Wikipedia, including photographs of translucent or greyish-white gelatin blobs that apparently evaporate shortly after having 'fallen'. According to folklore going back to the 14th century, it was believed to have been deposited on the Earth during meteor showers. Other explanations range from the jelly being the remains of toads, or worms, to the by-products of cyanobacteria and the paranormal. Sounds a bit like ectoplasm to me, that the Victorians obsessed about. Mind you, Melanie Reid in an article in The Times Online entitled: *Nature 1, Science 0 as finest minds fail to explain star jelly,* wondered whether it could be the remnants of a meteor shower, regurgitated frogspawn, fungus – or, less romantically, the gel from disposable nappies. She also asked if it could be evidence of extraterrestrial life, or perhaps the fallout from top-secret attempts by scientists to manipulate the weather![iii]

I love reading things like that. Whether there is any truth behind this tale is less important than the frisson. And my frisson over the Lake of the Woman is rather pungent. I suppose that what I feel in just thinking of that name is my own psychological equivalent of Star Jelly. At the moment I'm smoored with it. Or maybe I'm just oozing with ectoplasm. I can't imagine how thick and icky it will get when I turn my gaze to look at...

The lake that Judith told me about. The *Miroir aux Fees*. This wondrously named lake has a very different but equally bloody story.

Legend has it that seven sister faeries, who vowed to never go up to the surface in daytime in order to avoid mortals, once inhabited the lake. However, the youngest faery broke her vow and fell in love with a young knight who hunted by the lake. Her sisters eventually discovered her little secret and set off to catch and killed the young man. The young faery soon discovered what her sisters had done, and used all her magic powers to punish them. She cut their throats in order to recover some of their blood, which she mixed with her own blood, then threw them back in the deep of the lake. She then rushed to the young man and poured some of this blood elixir in his mouth and revived him. Her love for her knight was so strong that she abandoned her magic powers to become a mortal and left with him. Her sisters' blood kept flowing for seven days and nights; it flooded the surrounding woods and villages and dyed the soil in red.

Today, the surrounding forest is so dense that its surface remains perfectly still and reflects the surrounding trees and sky in the manner of a mirror – *miroir*. It is believed that the faeries who inhabit the lake come out at night and peer at their own reflections...

I don't suppose anyone reading this book will need reminding that the faeries talked about are not the cute little winged mites dancing among the daisies with bluebells for caps. We have to blame the Victorians for that. Think of the faeries, or the Fae, as a parallel line of evolution in a differing dimension, accessed by a crack between the worlds that curves slightly away from ours. In the Celtic tradition they exist in the Land of the Ever Young where there is no present, past or future. It is also said that within their realm there is no suffering, only degrees of joy, beauty and wisdom. However, some seers feel that the Fae lack free will and because of that they are unable to evolve. They are not always congenial to us humans because of the damage we have done to their realm. They can enchant, keep you enthralled, and lead you on a merry dance until you lose yourself – on more than one level.

In fact 'Faerie' could also be another name for the Invisible World itself, and in that sense the each-uisg or the kelpies connected with Loch na Mna can, in the broadest of terms, be regarded as creatures of the faery realm. And there are all sorts of Beings out there – or rather *in* there – that defy categorisation or even description.

Recently, an Irish seer using the name Acushla, working in Bath, told me that I was surrounded by faeries. Of course I should have asked her what they wanted, but I was too busy processing (on the little cinema screen before my brow), the other information she had given, and the moment passed. The faery realms fascinate me, as faery realms are apt to do to everyone. With respect to the *Miroir*, in particular, then if I'd been young and daft I'd be tempted to dive right in, magically. I created a single pathworking of my own once, in which I 'entered' Llyn Cau, which is a glacial lake two-thirds of the way up the Welsh mountain Cadair Idris, said to be one of the hunting grounds of Gwyn ap Nudd and the Wild Hunt. However I got scared and withdrew quickly, closing down and returning to the mundane world as soon as I could. I don't know what scared me, but I won't go in there again.

I say this because any attempts to link with Faerie should not be seen as a game. Remember, they are not our 'little helpers' and as I said earlier, by many accounts large portions of them really don't like us. At one time, in some hazy Ancient of Days, there seems to have been a Human-Faery Covenant which has long since been broken – by us. How you deal with this fracture is part of your own Quest. And if you enter areas (earthly or spiritual) that you think might be Faery territory, ask permission first.

A few years ago, sitting by a stunningly beautiful and monstrously quiet Welsh lake that my wife and I had only reached with extreme difficulty after endless obstacles, we both felt that the overwhelming Presence of the lake really did not want us. I had planned to do some (very simple) Elemental magicks up there and leave an offering in its depths but instead we left, very quietly. Our way back down was effortless, without any of the bewildering obstacles we had battled on the way up, and a stranger in an old Land Rover Discovery even turned up off the beaten track 'as if by magick', and gave us an easy route back into town. I don't think the driver was a Fae, but you never know.

I said in the beginning of this Journal that I would show how anyone can make an adequate inner pilgrimage without having to physically uproot themselves and get on buses, trains and planes and cross continents. So in case I've bigged myself up too much I really must talk now about how each person, no matter where they are, can reach their own Lake of the Woman or Faery Mirror.

In fact it is very easy. Or rather, it is easy in principle, but it does need effort. Without effort, then you're just wasting your time and indulging in what might be called Hobby Magick. There are two main approaches and so we can start with...

The Lesser Magick

Accept for a start, as a working hypothesis, that Wordsworth and other Nature Mystics are right, and that God is All and All is God. This segues neatly into my own favoured notion that All is One and One is All, which is the essence of Gnosticism, as I understand it. Not to mention the age-old Hermetic axiom of *As above, So below*. To which might be added *As without, So within*.

We are all parts of one infinite whole. I am you and you are me, so let's be kind to each other. For the purpose of this technique, adopt the ridiculous, mad, explosive, wonderful notion that there is no Past and no Future, and that all is happening *Now,* ever-becoming, infinite. What you might think of as past lives or future lives might well be accepted as 'other' lives. Those other incarnations, past and future, are living their lives *Now*, within you. And you are the people, the land, the country, the planet and the universe.

Of course, this will raise all sorts of considerations and questions beginning: 'Yes, but what about...?' To which I can give you no answer. I'm suggesting that you act 'as if' this were true, if only for a moment, or find some other paradigm that might work better.

Which means that Loch na Mna is within you, tucked away within a neat little Time Bud which floats in my psyche which is also your psyche. By visualising it, you bring it into being in a way that is relevant to you and you alone. Never mind that the 200 people actually living on Raasay today might see it as no more than an unexceptional body of water. You are taking its image and linking it with mythologies, and in so doing you will have the option of connecting with the energies and entities behind the myths.

There is nothing, these days, too absurd about this. If you go on-line you will find ten thousand souls offering path-workings involving places like Glastonbury Tor, Montsegur, Machu Piccu, Newgrange, the faery-haunted Eildon Hills, and a thousand sites across Europe, the Americas and Australia and, well, everywhere that humans have been touched by the innermost Mysteries within Nature.

Create your *own* path-working involving, say, Loch na Mna or the Faery Mirror Lake in Brittany. I emphasise this because other peoples' pathworkings rarely work for me, and because the more effort you personally apply, the more that inner beings will take note and decide if they actually *want* to make contact. Do research on-line. Buy detailed maps. Draw your own. Peer down at your chosen site using Google Earth. Imagine that this is going to be like the mirror in Alice's *Through the Looking Glass*. Choose an appropriate time when you won't be disturbed, set up your room in whatever way you feel appropriate, involving soft lighting, moon phases, incense, or soft music. Peer in as if it's a crystal ball. Step in. Dive in.

Very often, nothing might seem to happen. But the very fact that you are attempting something of this nature means that you are stepping aside from the worldly and heading toward the otherworldly. (It will always always work, though rarely when you want, and never exactly how you want. Stuff that I did 50 years ago is showing some very small blossoms now.)

Oh – and don't do drugs.

Having tried all that, you can also practice what I think of as…

The Greater Magick

I must disappoint you if you expect me to talk about robes and chanting and ceremonies and Cups and Swords and Wands and all the other paraphernalia that you might find in the High Church or in one of the legendary Magical Orders like the Stella Matutina. I'm not knocking or mocking such things. I know a number of magicians who like to get the togged up in this way and give it the Works, in a manner of speaking, though that's never appealed to me. You don't need a Chalice – you've got your cupped hands. Your single finger is a perfect Wand.

Perhaps you live in a run-down area. I certainly have, many times and in several countries. There is nothing to be ashamed of, ever, and you must *never* apologise to others. If your own dwelling is modest, as long as you keep it clean and tidy (Gawd, I sound like my mother!), it's as much a temple as any of the soaring structures you'd find among the Freemasons or the High Churches.

There is near me the large site of an old defunct factory. 20-odd years ago it used to make pies for most of England and Wales but then fell on hard times and was abandoned. Although the council has perpetual plans for rejuvenating it, nothing seems to happen, and the weeds grow bigger.

Weeds, as someone defined them once, are just misplaced flowers. The old man-made factory with its brick and steel, cement and concrete is dead and decaying but even the thinnest, puniest grasses can be seen muscling these substances aside as they reach up toward the sun. One day these will also push up through your own bones or ashes.

Just observing these little clumps, wherever they are, even on the pathways of your own garden, can thrill you with the absolute power of Nature. And if you can look at the most shrivelled, battered trees and shrubs cracking their way up through the ground in these places, and have a sense of them as purposive, intelligent beings in their own right, then you're touching upon the Greater Magick.

You can do this for the plants in your apartment. Your neighbours' window-boxes. Your local parks and playing fields. Try to have some sense of what Dylan Thomas described as 'The force that through the green fuse drives the flower...' in the poem that made him famous. That single opening line immediately connects nature and humankind: the energy apparent in a delicate flower is also present in us. We are one and the same because of this force. And it brings us both life and destruction. Which brings me back to the solid Mysteries of Nature and the sheer impermeable Magick of the Land.

In the most run-down areas you can get a sense of what lies behind the wastelands that Humans have, unintentionally created. There is a strong movement these days, in Britain at least, aimed at Rewilding. This is defined as a large-scale restoration of ecosystems where nature can take care of itself. It seeks to reinstate natural processes and, where appropriate, missing species – allowing them to shape the landscape and the habitats within. I'm all for that, but I would add another layer and suggest that we all try *re-enchanting* our locality.

Really, you can do this on your own.

I wouldn't worry about ley-lines, and this is why...

Some years I stood by the side of the River Avon and watched the full moon send a slim beam of light across the water to my very feet. But the thing is, everyone else along the river bank was seeing the same thing. Which means that, if you could see as everyone at the same time, the whole world was covered with this light, but as individuals we can only seen a sliver.

So with ley-lines, the whole world is under the flow of their energies, and you really don't need to pilgrimage to so-called Places of Power. It is all there, under your feet, everywhere and always.

It would also be fun, instructive, and genuinely magickal to perceive your own Earth Zodiac or 'Temple of the Stars' from sites within your own area - even if you live in the Rust Belt of the U.S. It will be just as valid as that discerned by Katharine Maltwood (and then hugely modified by Mary Caine), around Glastonbury – though I won't win too many friends in saying that. It's all about making an effort, and preferably *original* effort.

Just keep quiet about your Work and don't make a fool of yourself. It's old-fashioned, I know, but Eliphas Levi's injunction that the magician should Know, Will, Dare and above all **Be Silent** is still relevant.

I couldn't sleep last night and so was downstairs at 4 am reading on-line Raasay newsletters from a decade ago. One of them described a visit by ex-residents to a long abandoned village.

> Those of you who've been to Umachan will know the remoteness of the site, the steepness of the path, the few small green patches where cultivation must have been possible, and the ruins now surrounded by bracken. Our family was there for nearly eighty years; some of their neighbours for even longer. We gathered this summer to remember the forces that put them there; we celebrated their survival in such a hostile place and re-established our connection to this wee part of northwest Scotland.[iv]

Again, before this project I had no idea that Raasay had *any* history, and the description of that melancholic but immensely proud visit to Umachan made me sad. It's obvious that the islanders have a profound sense of Nature's power and ultimate triumph. I don't know why I felt sad. Perhaps it's because many of us have 'time buds' connected with our childhoods. So when, as adults, we revisit certain places and see the changes, we get maudlin about things that have been lost, and the infinite might-have-beens.

While I was on-line I ordered the Ordnance Survey map of the island and the autobiography of some chap who grew up there. I'm clearly going to have to do Work of my own with respect to Raasay. At the moment, Morgana le Fay and the nine priestesses on the Île de Sein are hidden behind thick mists and I think I've lost my direction.

Chapter 3

October 9th

Anasty sort of day, though it started out well, waking as usual with the 'time bud' of Raasay at the forefront of my musings and trying to keep it wrapped in a cozy image of something seen afar. But then we discovered that Water was trickling down through the ceiling of our spare room from a leak in our roof, and *then* found that flames were roaring up from the windows of the house next door. Fortunately the young couple and their children are safe and we're all rallying around. The street is full of firefighters.

In that book I glimpsed in the Samye-Ling monastery, one of the magicians stated that everything that happens – *everything* – can be seen as a 'secret dealing' between your innermost spirit and your Gods. Or something like that: the waves of the years have washed away the word-perfect details. It's certainly a notion that I've cleaved to for most of my life, but what I've learned this morning from the Waters and Fires and their fighters, is that if I have to choose between opening my Time Bud or helping the neighbours, then the bud can go rot.

Our neighbours are safe and staying with friends, though their house seems to have been gutted. No-one yet knows what caused the Fire. As for us, we've got a bucket under our ceiling catching the Water. I don't want any disasters, now, relating to Air or Earth, to make up the quaterrnity. With one eye and two somewhat-impaired ears alert for any danger, I'm trying to get back to my theme and create a clear path toward Brittany.

I would explain that when I had the first stirrings of this project some months ago, I was going to call it *Muirgen* – and I might yet do so. As I understood, the name Muirgen actually means 'sea born', and that this was the origin of Morgana le Fay. I can't remember where I got this information from, but it was probably the late Christine Hartley who was one of my teachers. And who, I would point out, channelled energies of Morgana le Fay during some of her inner workings in the late 1930s and 40s – though they didn't use that term then.

It strikes me though, that Raasay itself is 'sea-born', as are all islands, but I'll have to shove that notion aside for the nonce. And if all rain is ultimately 'born of the sea' then I'll have to stop Muirgen dripping down the walls into our spare room past the light switch and making a right mess of the carpet. I'm sure there's a magickal lesson or a 'secret dealing' there, but it's a damned nuisance.

We had planned to set off tomorrow to visit Pistyll Rhaeadr, some 180 miles away, Britain's tallest single-drop waterfall, in the very heart of Wales. Because of the problems with our roof and the torrential rain, and the obvious need to get it fixed, we decided to postpone our visit until Spring. I suppose this is one of those things of which we'll eventually say: It wasn't meant to be. Yet when my wife showed me the website some months ago my first reaction toward the place was: *Where have you been all my life?*

So just look at this: *www.pistyllrhaeadr.co.uk/index.html*

The whole area seems to be deeply impregnated with Celtic magick and the oldest deities and I felt that somehow, within the tumbling waters, I might get a glimpse of the Welsh aspect of Morgana and her two sisters, whom I hope to talk about soon.

The name *Rhaeadr* seems to be a combination of two words: *dwr* meaning water and *Rhea,* the goddess. So these are the waters of Rhea – which, incidentally, was one of the affectionate names given to 'Dion Fortune' within the closed confines of her lodge. As to the goddess herself you might want to track her down if she calls to you.

The writer of the website, who also seems to be the owner of the remote, siren-like tea-rooms at the falls' foot, waxes lyrically about the Iron Age forts on top of the Berwyn Mountains from whose range the waters tumble, the standing stones called after Gwyn ap Nudd (the king of the underworld), and viewpoints named in honour of the great Arthur of the Britons, plus what he describes as the dragon energies. Clearly, the whole area is alive with legend and myth. He adds:

> Here in this small and sacred spot; people understood about living with a spiritual connectedness to the land they lived on. Their ceremonies and rituals were about giving thanks for the fertility that the land gave them; the giving of daily prayer in the recognition of the unseen and eternal forces that these peoples knew about. We know the Celts revered both landscape and sun and moon. The land was the mother, the matron who provided all things essential for life. Where the shape of hills could be perceived as a sacred landscape they were thus named and revered.

Before he goes on to talk about the Llanrhaeadr Dragon, he suggests:

Those with an imaginative eye will want to watch the falling water to see if you too can discover the lady of the waterfall and the guardian of the falls, a monk in his long robes. She hides her skirts behind the longest drop of water and drops her long hair in front of her face. Certainly if you look long enough, all sorts of shapes will emerge. Allow yourself to be mesmerised by the continuously changing pattern of water and the spirit of the falls emerges.

I will certainly allow myself to be mesmerised when I get there. In fact I'm mesmerised now, 180 miles and probably six months away. If the chap who wrote that is not a Druid then I'd be very surprised, as his writing shows a truly deep connection with ancient things. No need to Re-wild or Re-enchant the Berwyn Mountains: they will do that to us.

I have to talk about Names and their power now, before I get tied down with Raasay or yet find myself winging my way toward Brocéliande. I'll try and show how everyone reading this can – *should* – create a Secret Name for themselves.

When you think about it, if you can't put a name to a person, object, place, time or experience, then you'll exist in a realm of absolute nothingness until you can create the Word of what's around you. And because he's just floated into my head I suppose I should begin by talking briefly about one of the least-known but most powerful of all the Irish magicians...

Many years ago Christine Hartley, 'an Adept if ever there was one', gave me the typescript of what she called *Kim's Book*, written in the late 1930s by a man using the pseudonym 'FPD'. This has been published in various sources since as *The Old Religion - a Study in the Symbolism of the Moon Mysteries*. It is an essay in several parts, and effectively a manual of self-initiation - as well as one of the finest essays on the realms of the Fae that I have read in my long life. I think I should include it in the appendix to this book, whatever form or title it will eventually take. FPD referred to the motto of the Seymour family, being *Foy Pour Devoir*. His full name and title was Lieutenant-Colonel Charles Richard Foster Seymour, and although he thought of himself as a Galway man his family seat, as they thought of it, was in Killagally in county Offaly. He died in 1943 at the age of 63.

Oh but I do like the thought of a battle-scarred and decorated soldier being such a deep explorer of the Faery Realms! And – ye gods and all their little fishes – he couldn't half write about Magick and Mysticism with a fluency and depth that few since have ever achieved.[v]

Christine, who was his priestess and *shakti* for many years (although no *physical* sex ever occurred between them), called him Kim, and the Name she used for herself within the magickal lodge was *Frere Ayme Frere*, which was also *her* family motto, passed down through the generations.

As members of the Hermetic Order of the Golden Dawn, whose details had leapt at me from the pages of Francis King's book, they all used what they called 'Magical Names', that tended to be traditional mottoes. 'Dion Fortune' as most of you probably know, was a contraction of *Deo Non Fortuna*, which was the family motto of the Firth family.

This is all very glamorous – or it seemed to be when I was young – but there is another level of perception needed. In that era between the two World Wars and just after, the genuine, highly-trained and disciplined Adeptii of the *real* Magickal Orders, connecting psychically with exalted Beings, knew how to wield Power; they had all the inner talents you would expect. But...they could also be insufferable snobs.

I said before that you should *never* be apologetic about where you live. Nor should you ever be apologetic about your background, whether posh or poor, privileged or disadvantaged. I'm not sounding like my Mam now, as she was an insufferable *inverted* snob, gawd bless her.

Whatever your background, you need to create a Magical Name, though perhaps we should think of it as a *Secret* Name to work with in your Secret Dealings.

For a start, I've never liked the name 'Alan Richardson'. Its syllables aren't smooth and I'm always reminded of a wheelbarrow being dragged across a cattle grid. I have a certain regret that when I was young I never chose a pen-name for myself, but that's another story. Besides, 'Alan Richardson' doesn't express my highest principles and impulses.

Think for a moment of what your Self would be like on the best and most inspirational day you ever had. Then try to find a Name that might express this. It could in fact be a motto of the sort I've just expressed. Or it could be an acronym. Or some random collection of sonics that just pops into your head. Create a little, simple ceremony or act in which you name yourself, while imbuing your thoughts – and feelings – with your highest aspirations. Whisper it to trees, into caves, or cracks in the ground, or above the waters of a lake. Show imagination.

And that's it, for starters. Of course, as your aspirations evolve, so will your Name change. But don't tell ANYONE what it is. This is your own 'secret dealing' with inner energies and entities. It is a means of communicating with your Self and other Selves.

Kim, I must confess, seems to have overshadowed me during some crucial years, although I always had him in my mind as the Colonel, rather than the familiar 'Kim'. Then, I wrote *Dancers to the Gods*, that contained the juxtaposed Magickal Diaries of himself and Christine as they worked under the aegis of the Fraternity of the Inner Light, before joining (I think) the Amoun Temple of the Golden Dawn. I reckon that he can explain the irrational rationale of what I'm trying to do here better than me, so dipping into my own copy now I'd like to quote from Kim's Book:

> Let the motto of the would-be Magus be: *Labor omnia vincit*. Act and react to these inner representations until you have lost all sense of *how* and *when* and the *where* in the feelings spontaneously created within you by these visions which have been so often built up mechanically by daily mental toil. When this happens a re-presentation is no longer just your subjective mental picture. It has become (for you) an entity which is not only objective but also vibrant with life, and it is real upon its own plane of being, though that is not this material plane of sensation.

Labor omnia vincit. Work conquers all. This is from a poem by Virgil and was written in support of Augustus Caesar's 'Back to the land' policy, aimed at encouraging more Romans to become farmers. (I was a little startled when, out of sheer curiosity, I googled the motto of the Richardson family, and although there were five variations, the first result was: *Labor Omnia Vincit*. There is no way, however, that I want to think of myself as Frater LOV, as would have happened if I'd joined one of the temples of the Golden Dawn.)

That's a bit dry, taken out of context, but in another essay Seymour also noted:

> 1. Man is the centre of concealed and potent forces; and
> 2. the unseen forces of Nature are of the same kind as those that exist in the soul of man.[vi]

I mentioned earlier the 'solid Earth stuff' that is far more important than trying to connect with dubious exalted beings from the vasty deeps. And by 'dubious beings' I do mean Masters, Mahatmas, Secret Chiefs, Maha Chohans, Manus, Gods and Goddesses, Archangels and all the rest. I'm not doubting the very existence of these, but I think we can learn to look at them – and connect with them – in a way that is not fawningly reverential.

But while I think on...

I mentioned earlier that dreadful word 'entity'. This conjures up all sorts of demonic notions. Yes, there are indeed malign and noxious energies on the inner planes that might be described as 'evil' and that can give you a jolt. Then again, if you were to walk around the centre of a busy town on a Friday night, there is always the possibility that you might stumble into some nutter and get mugged. Either avoid such places completely, or else take appropriate precautions. That might seem a bit cavalier of me, but if you have any kind of inner fire then you really must do the Work. Then, I promise, the information you need to progress will flit toward you like moths to the flame, and from every direction.

When it comes to the question of Evil I have no pat answer. I've heard that term used to describe Morgana le Fay, Set, Pan, Cernunnos and a host of other archetypal beings that I'm rather fond of. A couple of fundamentalists have said the same about me personally and there might be a smidgin of truth in that - from their viewpoint. One man's saint is another woman's sinner. I think it's something you have to work out yourself. Again, thanks to the internet there are thousands of sites that will give you good instruction in what might be termed 'psychic protection'. You might want to have some at hand if you do dive into Fae realms, whether in Raasay or Brittany.

I can hear water dripping into the bucket upstairs. I think I'd rather deal with a couple of small demons than this. The job needs scaffolding and very long ladders, neither of which I have, so I've summoned/ invoked the brilliant, legendary, and somewhat elusive Being known throughout West Wiltshire as Ryan the Roofer to come and deal with this, but he's very busy at the moment.

Chapter 4

October 17th

It didn't rain last night, so we didn't have to listen to Muirgen making a waterfall into the plastic bucket in the next room, or getting up at intervals to make sure the ceiling there hasn't collapsed. Today is dry, warm, and as I watch the sun sneaking through the curtains, I must confess that I'm still bemused and slightly enchanted by the gravitational pull of Raasay.

I read last night that the island is composed of the oldest rocks in Britain, and I wonder if that plays a part. I suppose the screen of my laptop has become an electronic Loch na Mna as I found myself pouring over a geology report by J.D. Morton and A.S. Baird of the School of Earth and Environment, University of Leeds, in which they comment:

> ...An unusually wide range of lithologies is seen in close proximity, juxtaposed by large-scale faults, which allow nearly 3 billion years of Earth history to be condensed onto one small island

It is, they assure us, one of the most geologically diverse landmasses in the world. They even give a free downloadable poster showing all the rocks, fault lines and strata in different fleshy colours, and the long slim mass of Raasay looks naked and rather vulnerable, like one of those slaughtered, limbless carcasses you see dangling in butchers.

Wherever you live, on whatever continent, I suppose the rocks beneath must exert influences every bit as potent as those from the stars above. As any Native America sage would insist, although no-one can ever 'own' the land, it certainly can own us. And if you can relate to trees as purposive intelligent beings, then surely this is true of the rocks themselves.

One of the many nice things about getting old is that I can look back and see how various events in my life have spread out from a single stem, without me realising. That is, incidents that seemed to be totally unconnected, have proved to be like petals on opposite sides of the same flower, opened from a single bud. I'll try to explain...

On that walking holiday in which we first glimpsed Raasay, we stayed in a large, creaking house on the shores of a sea-loch, some 10 miles away. I won't say exactly where, in order to protect the place I'm about to describe, and I might be lying about the distance. Scanning the Ordnance

Survey maps for this area I saw that there were some 'cup and ring' markings in the area and I wanted to visit these.

Cup and ring markings are invariably prehistoric, and take the form of roughly circular depressions that have been ground into the stone, and the lines curving in marked and determined patterns around them. No-one can agree as to what these represented, and the ideas put forward range from them being maps of the world, maps of the stars, maps of local tribes, sites where fat was set alight for religion, means of invoking spirits, records of ownership or boundaries and so on.

I have no ideas myself, but I wanted just to run the fingers of my left hand over them. I think it's something to do with the functions of the Right Brain that most people are aware of. You don't need to trek and find ancient stuff like cup and ring markings. You can do it with any item – *any* item – in your own home. Even if it's just a cheap and nasty toy from a cracker that was first imagined, designed and then created in Hong Kong. Or do this with some admirable craftsmanship in piece of furniture from your local store. You can float into the creators' minds in gentle ways, and sometimes feel a curious kinship. I just wanted to do this with the prehistoric markings, if only to say Hello!

As it was, we couldn't find the carvings but on the way I was struck by what I can only call the sense of an Earth Giant peering above the loch. That's a term of convenience. I don't mean a great physical creature with arms and legs. I mean a massive portion of rock, a cliff face, looming hugely above the waters, with the cracks, fissures, and all sorts of other impermeable features suggesting to me an ageless face. If I'd still been keen on the Kabbalah I'd probably try to show off by calling it a Macroprosopus, which can mean 'Long Face' or even 'The Infinitely Patient One', but I think Earth Giant is simpler and better, even if it's a bit comic-bookish.

Of course there's a name for seeing this sort of thing – pareidolia. Seeing what you want to see, but which has no real existence. Yet if you look up images for the massive stones at Avebury Circle you will see that many visitors have seen faces expressed by what were hitherto thought of as unshaped lumps in the Wiltshire earth. Once you see them, you can't *not* see them. In a curious way the stones become enlivened – at least within yourself. One of the stones has been named (not by me) as the Thinker, or Philosopher. I saw this myself, before knowing about that name, and at times, out the corner of my eye, the massive stone almost quivered into life. I regularly say Hello to that one.

So the Giant's 'head' had me transfixed, though of course s/he had not the slightest interest in or cognizance of a tiny little finite speck like myself. Goodness knows how massive the 'body' was below the loch but that didn't matter. To me, the Giant had been gazing from the waters up into the heavens since the beginning of Earth Time. S/he had seen comets crash, the dinosaurs come and go, numerous Ice Ages, mammoths and sabre-toothed tigers getting hunted to extinction; humans hunting and gathering, then working with stone, then metals, then planting crops as the climate changed. S/he would have seen tribes, armies, empires rise and fall and Mankind take to the air.

Believe me, I wasn't having any cosmic visions or ecstatic spiritual revelations and there were no tongues of fire licking anywhere. I simply had a marked but wordless sense of contact with the energies behind, beneath and within that 'Head'. I did my best to say Hello but no more than that.

The truly odd thing is, we tried to find the cup and rings on another occasion and failed again, having a picnic instead. Once more, I was nourished by the same sense of contact. It was Margaret who pointed out that despite the views, it had been an extremely tedious, endless, uphill trek both days. I was startled by this. To my mind it was an easy, level walk. I got a bit huffy so she made me look at the map, and the undeniable contours showing very steep inclines. Yet I had no sense of effort, no awareness of belting along ahead of her and going up long slopes.

Perhaps it was the Head's gift to me. Perhaps I'd been turned into a Celtic *lung-gom-pa*, bouncing along on the Earth's energies. Abbot Akong Tulku Rinpoche might have been proud of me.

And the point of this yarn is that I realised something today: the rock entity with whom I'd been having a simple commune was comprised of the same folds of rock that shoved up above the seas to form Raasay. Perhaps this is why the link with Raasay is quite tangible.

Normally I've been waking every morning with an image of its Time Bud – of that long, mysterious island in the bitter Western sea. It's not offensive, or threatening, and evokes nothing worse in me than a gentle sort of melancholy. Usually I can go back to sleep. Yet I do still want to break free and head off toward the enchanted forests of Brocéliande and other places where I might find Morgana le Fay and others of her kind, especially on the Île de Sein that I'll describe before too long – I hope! In fact I got another email today from Judith Page, telling me apropos of *rien*, about the Cairn of Barnenez on the coast in Brittany. As with the Mirror of Faeries, I'd never heard of this either, yet it is one of the earliest megalithic monuments in Europe as well as one of the oldest man-made structures in the world. It is also remarkable for the presence of carvings far more sophisticated than the simple cup and ring stuff. The motifs include what some have interpreted as axe blades, bows, horned signs, and goddesses. But others have insisted that actually the horned signs are definitely birds and the goddesses certainly phalluses. I don't think I need to agonise about any pareidolia of my own when it comes to the Giant's Head.

'Brittany is full of secrets,' Judith's email concluded, 'and the Druids there make sure that nothing leaks out.'

Hmmmm...

Bizarrely, an awkward piece of flotsam has just drifted into my mind and I have to grasp it. I think it appeared because of my thoughts about Raasay being in the Mystick West, from my inner viewpoint; also because the website describing Barnenez locates it, (and numerous megalithic cousins) in what they term 'Great West France'. I've never heard of Brittany described as that before, but then again it's been many years since I visited.

What has popped up, almost embarrassingly, is the theme of an old movie: *Support Your Local Sheriff.*

I make no apologies for what might seem a crass insertion into the narrative, nor for being a lifelong fan of Westerns. The notion of the Wild West was my first love, and when I was five and growing up poor in a coal-mining town in Northumberland, I was certain of two things: that one day I would live in America (I did so, twice), and would also write the greatest co'boy book ever. Alas, I haven't quite got around to twirling my six-guns yet.

I must add, because I like any kind of challenge to orthodoxy, that historians have shown the Wild West was not very Wild at all. Dodge City, for example, in its bloodiest year, had just five killings in 1878. Of the 250,000 pioneers who set out across the West between 1840 and 1860, only 362 died in violent contact with Indians (am I allowed to use that term?) While only 426 died on the Indian side. 'More usually Indians sold food and horses to the travellers, and provided guides in return for useful goods.' [vii]

Of course, those details won't bother me at all when it comes to my opus. I think it was Mark Twain who said 'Never let the truth get in the way of a good story', so I'll take heart from that when I put on my spurs and polish my Buntline Specials.

So the point of *this* ramble is that the main character, played by James Garner, is travelling **West** and only passing through the town of Calendar, Colorado, on his way to Australia. Every attempt to leave and head toward the antipodes is benignly thwarted by need, happen-stance and falling in love within the town and with the town itself. At the end, as narrated by Jack Elam, we learn that he stays within Calendar and never gets to Australia – but he reads about it a lot. It's a cheery fillum, and it makes me wonder if this is to be my lot with respect to Raasay. There could be worse fates, but we'll see.

As I write this, the postie brings me my large-scale Ordnance Survey map of the island and I spread it out on our table, covering most of the surface. I haven't yet ordered a map of Brittany but I suppose I must do so quickly to counteract the pull. Maybe I'm being dragged down by the literary equivalent of a kelpie. Or maybe the Earth Giant just wants to hang onto me for a little while longer.

When you think about it, maps are a useful part of the inner process. Every fantasy tale worth its salt is preceded by a map showing where everything is about to happen: *The Hobbit, Lord of the Rings* and *Game of Thrones* to name just three. I can pore over maps as blissfully as I can read a good book, though when it comes to translating what I see on map into where I should walk on the ground, then I'm famous for getting pixie-led.

My children call me (with heavy irony) Pathfinder Richardson, on account of the number of times I've got myself lost. Maybe describing myself as pixie-led is just a glamorous and slightly inaccurate term for me being a hopelss map-reader.

I love to see the Gaelic names that spring out though: *Meall Daimh, Eilean an Inbhire, Glac Dhorca, Glas Eilean...* I don't know what any of them mean. There are lots of place names in English too, but they don't have the same attraction. The Scottish Gaelic has always evoked a lovely song within my mind even though I don't understand the words, whereas the Welsh names on a map are like those spiky things the police throw across the road to stop speeding criminals.

I was gently surprised to see, too, a small and obscure area of Raasay that has an obscure name highly relevant to my family. In this age of on-line security I won't mention it in case my bank account gets plundered. I can only say, on seeing this...*Hmmmm.*

Did my family, going back through the centuries, have some connection here? I've no idea. My mother – my Mam – told me that *her* mam (who died before I was born) was a 'Scotchie', and was fey. A talent which terrified my Mam. I have no intention of trying to research my family tree to see if it would take me back into the Highlands and Islands. I no longer get excited by the idea of sacred or familial bloodlines, any more than I do about about ley-lines.

In the light of what I said about Magickal Names and Secret Names, I did have the notion this morning that I should try and find out the meaning of the name Moluag in case it has been trying to impart knowledge to me (and therefore us) all along…

His original name in Celtic seems to have been *Lughaidh*, which would have been pronounced as Lua. As his fame grew (I'll come to that later) they added the prefix *mo*, as a kind of honorific, and the suffix *ag*, as an apparent endearment. Using on-line but modern dictionaries, then in Irish *Lughaidh* means Remain, but in Scots Gaelic it means Reading – neither of which set my spirit alight. However, putting the name *Moluag* into the same, then in Scots Gaelic it means Pebble, while Irish translates it as Water Praise. This might refer to the legend of a rock (or pebble?) detaching itself from the Irish coast and bearing the saint across the waves to the island of Lismore, in Loch Linnhe, where he landed and began his mission. In my head, I think I'll just call him Lua, and see if he makes any kind of appearance.

But while I was on-line I thought I would finish my evening by also looking up Muirgen, and found it was the name of a shapeshifting female saint who was associated with the sea, while Morgana was from the Old Welsh Morcant, a compound name composed of the elements môr (sea) and cant (circle, completion) or can (white, bright). Morgen, in Old Breton, does indeed mean Sea-Born. I must admit a shapeshifting female saint excites me more than any male missionary saint, so I don't think Lua will snaffle my soul easily.

I do hope to balance the pair of them some day, though, even if they're oil and water and half a world apart.

Still no sign of Ryan the Roofer, but it has remained dry, with quite strong Winds that are apparently the tail-end of a monstrous hurricane in the far Atlantic. I'm not unduly anxious.

An odd thing today, though. Some anonymous soul sent me an old, battered copy of *Sacred Waters*, by Janet and Colin Bord. The sender knew the name of our street but got the house number wrong and it was

38

brought to me by a previously unknown young woman who introduced herself as Devina. I looked up that name too, and it means 'beloved, divine or heavenly'. Perhaps she was a Fae too, you can never tell. I thought I'd read all of the books by the Bords, but I was completely unaware of this one. As I do my morning whizz across town, easily achieving the 30 minutes of Brisk Walking urged by my Active 10 app, I'll take it with me to browse in the various cafes. I'm sure that somehow this will help me with the present book.

Chapter 5

October 20ᵗʰ

In the past few days there has been neither rain (Water), winds (Air) but quite a bit of warm sun (Fire), so I managed to attend to the Earth by strimming and mowing the grass for the last time before Winter sets in. There is a small, very old faery bell at the bottom of our garden that I salvaged from the enchanted cottage down Murhill, that featured in my novel *The Moonchild*. I gave that a few chimes after I packed the strimmer and mower away, and hoped the Fae heard.

Last night, on the edge of sleep, I felt inspired to visualise myself as Luaigh stepping onto a rock and being carried across the sea to Lismore, feeling the elements around me all the way. Nothing special happened and the day-dream (it was too light to call it a 'pathworking') simply petered out into totally irrelevant dreams.

This, I would guess, is probably what happens with most people, and should not in any way be regarded as failure. Of course you'll always get some heavy-duty magician saying you should have done it this way or that way, during a specific time and place, sitting or lying in particular posture with your hands just-so and your breathing regulated. On the many occasions in my youth when I did follow the heavy-duty advice to the letter, it was no more successful than dropping off to sleep. I wouldn't reject this approach off-hand, but as long as you put in the Work, you will find your own tidal rhythms. Fortunately, I've always had the kind of slow-burning madness that made me keep going, so that I was always 'on'.

I'm not saying that's good for *you*. I am saying, don't be afraid to find your own way of working, even if you feel like St Moluag travelling on ocean streams by standing on a small rock. Don't feel you're missing out if you see the heavy-duty magicians apparently surging past in their crystal barges on great Magickal Currents. Whether you accept Lua as an inner contact with someone from far away and long ago, or a simple metaphor that will encourage your own efforts wherever you live, then he is completely valid. In fact, as a metaphor alone, there's rather a pleasant ambience about him. I think I'm becoming fond of the lad.

And I can call him 'lad' because one of the on-line articles described how he lived to an 'extreme old age'. In fact when he died he was five years younger than I am now.

I wrote much earlier that I invited St Moluag into my house and psyche on the understanding that he/it didn't mess us about. I don't blame him for the troubles in our roof, because we were aware of a fault in the tiles last year but did nothing about it. I assumed he hadn't taken up the offer either because he wasn't interested or because, as an energy or entity, he was no longer around. Then I realised with some delight that, in a silly way, he'd been on the side of our fridge all along!

I'd better explain this too…

Not long ago (I forget the date), our town had its annual Apple Fayre, which coincided with the bimonthly Artisan Market in the main street and within the Town Hall. In the upper room of the latter (deeply symbolic, that!) were various stalls of highly skilled, hand-made crafts. I wasn't going to go up there but my wife insisted.
One of the stalls displayed the work of a young woman whose speciality was in highly-detailed engravings on wood. I'm not sure if 'engraving' is the right term: she burned extremely fine lines and patterns to create her images, using the textures of the wood to deepen the pictures.

Margaret and I were impressed; her work was beautiful. She had even made a complete set of Runes under the aegis of, I suppose, a local Rune Master or Mistress. She did explain, but I wasn't wearing my hearing-aid and so lost the details. I was tempted to show-off as usual by asking if they were *futhorc* and *futhark* runes but managed to keep my gob shut for once.[viii]

In the event I bought a little round fridge magnet that caught my eye. It was as much to support local talent as anything to do with a magickal fancy. The wood had concentric tree-rings, like the waves of the sea, and burned into it was a solitary, cloaked and hooded monk with staff in hand and his back to the viewer.

'That's you', my wife said, and I was slightly inclined to agree.

It was a couple of days later, when I remembered my invitation to Moluagh, that it suddenly struck me… This little and lonely priestly figure on the disk, with his big staff, was St Moluagh's calling card.

It was the staff that convinced me. Astonishingly, this is still in existence, and is known as Bacchuill Mór, 'the great staff', a piece of blackthorn 34 inches long and originally covered in a gilded copper case. It was preserved on Lismore, in Bachuil village, and is now in the care of the Livingstone family after having been, for some time, in the custody of the Dukes of Argyll. Because of their associations with the Bacchuill Mhór this Livingstone family holds the ancient title of *Barons of Bachuil*.

There is also – possibly - a large bell which *might* have belonged to him, that disappeared during the Reformation and was only found again much later. I would give a lot to run my left hand and right-brain over both those items. Not because I might get any psychic impressions and visions – I wouldn't - but simply to say *Hello.* And possibly *Thank you...*

Alistair Livingstone of Bachuil, holding the Staff of St. Moluag. His son Niall is the present Baron of the Bachuil.

He's taking over, isn't he?

I've moved the magnet from our fridge and put it on a piece of ironwork on our old fireplace, in the sitting room. It's a far more comfortable place, I'm thinking. But I have to say now that this little disk has no talismanic powers. It contains no 6th Century Celtic spirit. Nor will it attract any kind of veneration from me. It is just a fridge-magnet.

Am I being absurd? Yes *and* no. I'm acting 'as if'. I'm suspending disbelief. I'm throwing myself open to the possibility that everything happening is a 'Secret Dealing' between myself and unknown parts of my Universe.

It strikes me now, late evening and after a busy day, that when I do escape from Raasay long enough to write about Morgana and Muirgen, that for the large part I will be dealing with the infinite flexibility of Myths. It will be like clutching mist. Whereas dear Lua (remember, that's what the name Moluagh meant) – dear Lua and his very hefty skull-cracking staff was solid flesh and blood, even if he did get shrouded with a few gauzy legends. The only story about him that I don't believe is the one about him having a boat race across the Lynn of Lorn with St Mulhac.

The bet was that the first one to land on the isle of Lismore would have the right to found a monastery there. Realising that he was going to lose, Moluag cut off his finger and threw it ashore north of the broch of Tirefour, enabling him to claim victory.

I don't know anything about St Mulhac, the Lynn of Lorn, or the broch of Tirefour though I suspect I'll be googling them soon – probably in the wee small hours. But if I'm going to dive into the *misty* mythologies of the Sea-Born Queens when I voyage toward Brittany, then I must first give what tangible *earthy* history there is around Lua, and see what I can learn from him. Though I'm damn sure I'm not going to to use the title of Saint when I send my thoughts to the lad.

So…

He seems to have been born around 597. Again, no-one knows *where* he was born, but he certainly came to prominence at the massive monastery of Bangor in Ireland. Bangor Mór was named 'the great Bangor' to distinguish it from Bangor on the Dee in Wales, and was one of the greatest missionary centres of all time. It had been founded by Comgall, who instituted a rigid monastic rule of incessant prayer and fasting. Far from turning people away, this ascetic rule attracted thousands, including Lua. When Comgall died in 602, the annals report that three thousand monks looked to him for guidance. Bangor Mór was also known as the house of Perpetual Harmonies because of the continual singing, which was antiphonal in nature, based on the call and response of two opposing choirs, often singing alternate musical phrases from the Psalms. Bangor missionaries carried this to the continent in the centuries after Lua's time. By the 12th Century Bernard of Clairvaux spoke of Comgall and Bangor, stating, 'the solemnization of divine offices was kept up by companies, who relieved each other in succession, so that not for one moment day and night was there an intermission of their devotions.'

If you're inclined to that sort of thing, you can imagine the power, not to mention the beauty of hearing those Perpetual Harmonies, and if you're a participant then I do think you're likely to have moments of transcendence. Some years ago, long after my first and only glimpse of Raasay, my wife and I sat quietly in the back of Quarr Abbey on the Isle of Wight when the Benedictine monks were chanting their antiphons. Neither of us knew the Latin or had even the slightest sense of what it might mean, but we both burst into tears. This may have been a Past Life or Other Life thing going on within us, I really couldn't say; the purity of sound and cadence, wave after wave, smashed at our heart centres. A small part of me envied those fellas and I didn't see them as lonely, lost and perhaps tortured souls but as notes in some forgotten song.

And if you think about it, there is not a person reading this who has not at some time in their life been profoundly moved by music, whether it was deeply religious or Heavy Metal. You will have had moments, whether in your apartment or in your car or at a live gig or, (these days) walking along with earphones and oblivious to the outer world, when you felt swept up in a large wave, connected to something bigger than yourself and perhaps moved to tears also.

I don't think that Lua raced across a loch with Mulhac to get to Lismore first, but I do think that when he was in Ireland he was deeply inspired by the stories of a fellow monk known as Columcille, who died in the year Lua was born. In 563, Columcille and 12 companions had crossed the Irish Sea in a coracle, and landed on a deserted island now known as Iona (Holy Island). Eventually, Iona became the heart of Celtic Christianity and its existence was one of the strongest influences in the conversion of the Picts, Scots, and Northern English.

I was about to launch my literary curragh and briefly circumnavigate this figure of Columcille, who is better known as St Columba, one of the towering figures of Western spirituality. But as I sit here brooding on a grey day before I march briskly over to the dentists, I realise that Columba is the spiritual equivalent of Corryvrekan.

The actual Gulf of Corryvreckan is a narrow strait between the islands of Jura and Scarba, off the west coast of mainland Scotland. It is famous for its tidal currents and standing waves. The maelstrom which forms at the right state of the tide is the third largest whirlpool in the world.

Columba is that whirlpool. Believe me his energies will set you swirling, sucking you around and ever inward to that great vortex in the centre. Goodness knows where that might take you but it's somewhere very deep.

So I'll leave him be for a moment and get back to Lua, who would certainly have been inspired by his predecessor to convert the Highlands and Islands of what we now think of as Scotland, but they knew as Alba - just over the horizon from Bangor Mór…

Lua's journey in a curragh, or Irish skin boat, would have taken him past Corryvreckan in order to get to Lismore, which was the first stop in his mission. His first settlement was in the north of the island, close to a megalithic site surmounted by a high cairn which once marked the funeral pyres of Pictish Kings. Lua seems to have chosen that place because it was the sacred island of the Western Picts whose capital was at Beregonium, across the water at Benderloch. This was their holy place, and they were cremated according to their rites on that ancient man-made 'burial mound' of *Cnoc Aingeil* (Gaelic for 'Hill of Fire') at Bachuil.

Lismore was therefore the perfect place for a young lad still thrumming from inner heavenly choirs to begin singing. And it seems that, along with his fellow Celtic Christian priests, he chose to build upon the continuity between early Christianity and Paganism rather than attack the differences. It is usually assumed that the native Picts of this area practised some form of 'Celtic polytheism': a blend of Druidism and other sects. By every account the conversion process was one of gradual education rather than outright confrontation and there were remarkably few martyrs in that area.

As a gnosticky type of Pagan, I suspect these days that my ideas about Celtic Christianity are about as accurate as the Old West of the Hollywood movies.

The New Agey approach to *Celtic Christianity* has them as the good guys, with: women priests; full equality for women at every level; a sympathy for (if not actual belief in) reincarnation; profound herbal knowledge; the Two Sights; powers of spiritual healing. Plus a determination to work with and for the very lowest levels of society in the hope they might be inspired toward the Christ.

The New Agey approach to the *Church in Rome* has their male priesthood: regarding women as inferior; possibly without souls; temptresses. They sought to build their power by converting the local kings first, accumulating wealth, and enforcing the Christ upon the common people, the option always being 'Convert or Die'.

I suppose the two responses are bit like the antiphonal psalmody I mentioned earlier: two groups of different believers, separated by the much-trodden aisle of time, thundering across their own sacred hymns and trying to suppress the other but also convince themselves. Personally, I believe that if the Church of Rome hadn't triumphed at the Synod of Whitby in 664, which led to the eventual dissolution of the Church of Iona, then the world today would be a much nicer place.

You might want to research that yourself though, coz I can feel another kind of Corryvrekan swirling around me as two powerful currents collide between the narrow islands of my own prejudices.

I'm not sure why, but all that last has made me somewhat doleful. Maybe I've created a bit of a vortex.

However, our dear Lua was obviously successful in *his* mission. Remember that in his youth he was aching for the 'White Martyrdom', which seems pretty fierce and joyless to me. But if he lived to 'extreme old age' he might have bypassed all that nonsense and spent his years among the Highlands and Islands being kind to himself as well as others. Before too long after his arrival on Lismore chapels dedicated to him sprang up in north Skye, Tiree, Mull, Pabbay and our Raasay itself, with the mother church remaining on the island of Lismore, where he became bishop. Very many more were dedicated or at least connected with him, but some were re-dedicated to other saints when Scotland became Roman Catholic, or otherwise after the Reformation. In many cases it is difficult to say if one or another church was originally erected by Lua himself or by one of his disciples of the first or second generation. Some people feel he should be regarded as the true Patron Saint of Scotland rather than St Andrew, but that's beyond my remit here. There is an excellent short piece on You-Tube putting the case for that, and you'll also hear his name pronounced correctly.[ix]

I wonder what he would feel if he could read Raasay's *Community Newsletter* for July 2016, as I did on-line just now.

Hallelujah! St Columba's Portree, St Mary's Sleat and St Michael & All Angels' Raasay have a new priest! St Columba's church was packed as over a hundred folk from many denominations (in itself a cause for great joy) came together to rejoice in Rosemary Bungard's ordination last Saturday. Bishop Kevin, in his inimitable style, set the mood of celebration, causing gales of laughter with a few well-chosen words.

I like the sound of Bishop Kevin. He then gave an inspiring sermon based upon what Rosemary had said to him when she started her 'unending journey': *I am a work in progress.* To which Kevin replied that we are all works in progress, as there are no clocks in Heaven - which I thought rather artful of him. After the sermon Rosemary's daughter, Elita Poulter, played the Adagio from Bach's violin sonata no.1 in G minor most exquisitely. Then her son sang Cesar Franck's *Panis Angelicus*. Everyone was moved. The clergy then laid their hands on Rosemary in blessing and prayer and the Bishop anointed her. She was vested with a chasuble and handed a Bible and the chalice and paten prepared for her first Eucharist.

> As the final flourish Neil Colquhoun, the organist, played a stirring and gorgeously uplifting Hallelujah Chorus from Handel's *Messiah* in which we all attempted to join! A magnificent buffet was provided to feast our bodies after the wonderful feast for the soul.

I am sure that Moluag himself would have liked Bishop Kevin's ready wit and thrown all thoughts of a 'White Martyrdom' aside in his dash toward the buffet. But more importantly, 1500 years after his own mission, he might have joined in with more than a few Hallelujahs of his own at the sight of the first woman priest (a wife and mother of two) now ministering in his Isles.

Now, I think I need to crash out...

Chapter 6

October 24th

I've still got this slight frisson of sorrow after peering into the notions of Celtic Christianity as opposed to Roman Christianity. Maybe the problems with our roof are somehow symbolic: perhaps there are a few things slightly misaligned within me that allow the rain to enter. And how is this relevant to my notional reader in the middle of a land-locked state on the other side of the Atlantic? As to that, I would suggest that we all have moments of reflection when we fear the things we have earnestly believed might not be as true as we needed and hoped. Or that people and philosophies once scorned might show glimmerings of unsuspected goodness. I think there's a metaphor here involving Lua's staff: we can sail through life clutching something that is powerful, often using this to fight off assailants or else give support when we're a bit wobbly. I don't necessarily mean hard-core religious divides: it can relate to individuals we know, or our parents. I'll have to think on that. I don't meditate, incidentally, as that doesn't work for me either: I just have good Thinks, usually in a local café after a brisk walk. Outwardly I will seem to be reading the newspapers, but inwardly my thoughts do the bobbing cork thing.

Margaret is working in London today. It's pouring there, but rather sunny and properly autumnal here, as it has been for a few days.

Thinking of London (where I used to live), I'm somehow reminded of when the great French magus Eliphas Levi made his first visit there in 1854, both to escape from 'certain family troubles' and give himself up, without interruption, to science. *By* 'science' he meant that he intended to summon, stir and evoke to visible appearance the spirit of Apollonius of Tyana. He described this in detail in his influential *Dogme et Rituel de la Haute Magie,* and if you like magick with all the bells, candles, chants, weaponry, incense, incantations and robes, then you might want to find that book on-line[x]. If you do, be prepared to be pleasantly surprised by how down to earth and practical the man was, and not at all en-glamoured by the very process of evocation.

I've decided today, however, that I'm going to attempt a very similar evocation. I'm going to use all the modern Arts Magickal of land-lines, mobile phones, internet and snail-mail to summon, stir and evoke to physical appearance the very substance of Ryan the Roofer, who seems to be moving in very mysterious ways across the other rooftops of Wiltshire but not toward ours.

A thought just struck me: is there such a being as a Patron Saint of Roofers? To my surprise, there is: Saint Vincent of Saragossa, Spain. A martyr, he was apparently fearless and had an unusually high threshold of pain, and so chose the harder more difficult path when tested. His body was stretched, subjugated to high extremes of heat, his skin was cut and burned and he was placed in uncomfortable painful positions. I'm not going to go down on bended knee to him, but he's got to be worth a shout isn't he? This is the sort of 'science' Eliphas Levi meant. I'll let you know how this works out too.

Then another thought struck me: What is St Moluagh patron saint of? Googling that, I learn that by popular tradition in Lewis in the Outer Hebrides, the very name of St. Moluog was invoked against madness, and many lunatics were healed there.

I suspect I'll come back to that point later.

October 26th

I woke at 4 this morning with the term 'Fata Morgana' in my mind. So I really must try and get back on track with my original project. Mind you I'll be distracted because in two hours time England will be playing New Zealand in the semi-finals of the Rugby World Cup, and I must watch that, even though I have little understanding of the rules.

By and large the Welsh, Scottish and Irish supporters loathe the English and are always happy to see us stuffed. For myself, I'm equally supportive of them if England aren't involved, but they probably hate me for that. With my astonishing powers of far-seeing I predict New Zealand to win by 2 points.

Fata Morgana…I don't know why this crept into my thoughts enough to wake me. Is she trying to tell me something? A Fata Morgana is a mirage. In fact a superior mirage that is often photographed, and usually seen as a narrow band right above the horizon. It's an Italian term named after Morgana le Fay from a belief that these mirages were fairy castles in the air, or false land created by her witchcraft to lure sailors to their deaths. These mirages significantly distort the object or objects on which they are based, often such that they are completely unrecognizable. A Fata Morgana may be seen on land or at sea, in polar regions, or in deserts. It may involve almost any kind of distant object, including boats, islands, and the coastline. Often this special mirage changes rapidly and can comprise several inverted and erect images that are stacked on top of one another. I suppose the idea of the Fata Morgana has come into my head to help me get clarity on the Sea-Borne priestess herself.

Writing about Moluagh has been easy because there is plenty of hard information about him, and plenty of earthy connections to give him shape. There are even images of him created centuries after, so that light can come through him via stained glass and into his churches. Of course, whether these images are accurate is anybody's guess. I suspect not. They are individual artists' means of 'evoking to visible appearance', in a gentler, kinder but no less inspired version of what Eliphas Levi achieved with Apollonius of Tyana.

How do *I* see Morgana le Fay? Well, I would never for one moment trust my own 'far seeing' because despite my moment of clairvoyant clarity the England rugby team stuffed the near-invincible New Zealand 'All Blacks' 19-7. I sort of see her (or rather *feel* her) as the spirit that lay behind the young Christine Hartley for a time, as I'll detail later. Even so, looking at Google Images for this Sea-Borne woman, there are thousands of representations, almost all of them red or black haired, none of them

demure or kind, many of them intensely sexual, edged with darkness and – for me at least – irresistible. Maybe that's fae calling to fae. One of the few that isn't is one by William Henry Margetson (1861-1940) which makes her beautiful but rather drippy. Mind you, as I sit here at 4.30am musing on the much larger image on my pc, I think she might be helping me visualise her, or feel her ambience, though I've had to horizontally flip the picture to do so. There she is, innocently looking at the rising steam with her right brain, and stirring it with her wand into an uncanny shape. I was thinking of that when I made myself a cup of tea and watched the steam rising from our kettle and wafted it around. The water, the fire, the air... a thin and dissolvable version of Morgana created by the alchemies of the elements.

I think that all such images are, to an extent, personal *fata morganas* – things seen afar that are hazy in nature and never quite reachable, though I'm not in any way saying that such visions are inherently false. Later on, I really must get Christine Hartley and Colonel Seymour's Magical Diaries down from the loft and remind myself of the Work they did in that direction.

The clocks went back last night and this always throws me a little. I still don't see why we need to do this, but it must be something to do with the farmers and I'll certainly go along with them. In a moment I'll go back to sleep again for a wee while.

Mind you I did wake with a certain thrill because yesterday, in a highly liminal place in town (i.e. the doorway of Tesco's, our large supermarket), Ryan the Roofer finally appeared and confirmed that he would come and fix our roof within a few days. I'm not sure if it was the Art Magick I did or the prayer to St Vincent but I'm not knocking it. In the meantime, I'll invoke Morgana again via the kettle and take another cuppa tea and a KitKat up with me.

But... I feel compelled to recap before I do that. I'm feeling slightly tired and wobbly, a bit like Lua trying to cross the Irish Sea on a pebble, according to the legend – or is it a myth? Before I described my very first sighting of Raasay, my mind was already filled with the thought of Morgana, and I see in an old notebook which I got from Poundland that I've scribbled in large letters:

> *Morgana means either* 'Dweller of the Sea' *or* 'From the shore of the Sea'. *Or from Old Welsh* 'Morcant', *a compound name composed of the elements* môr (sea) *and* cant (circle, completion) *or* can (white, bright).

I've probably said that already. But why on earth am I trying to get toward Morgana le Fey, whose historical existence is as substantial as the steam I was whirling around from the kettle, using the wand of my finger? I don't know.

I'm off back to bed now, just as my wife is getting up.

October 28th

Margaret is away at the gym doing Body Combat and perfecting her flying sideways kicking. I'm sure that will be useful next time we go to Tesco's. Me, I've been buying peanuts and fatty balls for the birds in our garden. We've got a new bird-feeder thingy that pokes into the ground and looks a bit like an inverted, exploded version of John Dee's *Monas Hieroglyphica* which he felt embodied his vision of the unity of the Cosmos. We hang all sorts of goodies on it and watch every morning with delight as it creates the avian equivalent of a mass brawl. I wonder if there's a sedate, sad, grey-feathered granny-sparrow in our eaves watching all the havoc and comparing me, the human, to some war-mongering deity from the Dark Side.

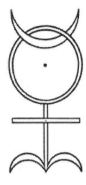

I must admit that the re-appearance of Le Fay into my psyche has created a differing ambience to that of Lua, which is not in any way inimical, but not particularly cozy. I've used that term 'ambience' several times before, relating to a feeling associated with place, person, or thing. Because it has floated into my my head again, then like an old druid seeing everything around him as omens or messages, I should try and explain...

You see I got a letter today from a friend of mine called Fran. She explained – almost apologised - that she was 'psythick' and so couldn't go deeply into the Otherness. I used to say the same about myself and always envied those who could see Spirits jostling as clearly as crowds in a football match. I was encouraged, recently, by stumbling upon the book *Seventh Sense* by Lyn Buchanan, a former (and very successful) Remote Viewer for American Intelligence. He argues that our sixth sense is ambience, while the psychic sense is then to be regarded as the seventh sense. The exercise he gives to develop this is simple enough. Beginning immediately, notice every doorway you go through. Before you do, stop and see if you can get a feel for the ambience in every room you are leaving. Then step through the door and see if you can feel the change in ambience. You don't need to try and describe it, but just aim at sensitizing yourself to finer and finer amounts of change in ambience.

This exercise should be done with *every* doorway you go through from now until you die. That means doors between rooms, entrance and exit doors in buildings, the bathroom door, the bedroom door, the car door, etc. *Every* doorway. At some point it will become second nature to you, and you will have added an entirely new dimension to your awareness, and therefore to your life. You will be as the sighted are in the land of the blind.[xi]

He estimates that probably 90 percent of the events and actions that pass for 'psychic' are nothing more than ambience.

Thirty years ago I began a phase of doing similar at every gateway, or edge of any woodland, visualising Merlin as the link between one realm and another, or else Cernunnos, or Morgana herself while standing at the edge of the sea. I suppose I still do this, but more usually with nameless figures of the Fae these days. This can be done by yourselves at any liminal place that you might feel is a point of transition, waiting, and not knowing, and where transformation might occur. For example, I'm something of a heretic in that I've no particular interest in Atlantis; yet when I've stood on the edge of the Marine Lake in Weston super Mare, or the very tip of Brean Down, watching the sun setting over the sea, I was swept by a energies of incredible age and tone (ambience!?) that could only really be described as Atlantean.

I'll come back to that Western-most place and energy in due course when I talk in more detail about Christine Hartley, but in my early days I didn't consciously build the concept of 'ambience' into any of my practices; yet this is perhaps more valid and certainly healthier than trying to provoke visions. I certainly used the technique in Brokerswood today, when playing Laser Tag on a team with three small grandchildren. The kids whizzed around like hornets to get at the enemy, and I made slow, stately, and quite majestic progress. I felt a bit like the ancient pharaoh Rameses II, running around the ritual boundary markers of his kingdom as part of the Sed festival, demonstrating his fitness to rule. As I made my stately way through the killing zones, soaking up the differing ambiences of the wood, I was shot to buggery. My team still won, despite me taking all the hits. I'm not sure what the dryads in the trees felt, but I did apologise.

I rarely did have actual visions when doing all this Work in the past but somehow, within, things often (though not always) woke up. And then came rushing out toward me like the sparrows from our eaves.

So...

53

Is there any hard information about Morgana le Fay? Is she no more than mythological imagery within the mind that can get ensouled by the magician? Was she – *is* she - connected with any actual *place*? I hope so, because I want to get back to the Earth-consciousness that really concerns me. I've been aware of her stories for so long that I've always taken her existence as an inner plane Being for granted. Here is as much as I need to express as regards her 'history'...

Morgana le Fay's first appearances in medieval literature were invariably as: a goddess, a fae, a witch, or a sorceress. She was originally seen as benevolent and was King Arthur's magickal saviour and protector. In later centuries the story-tellers made her a queen bitch as well as a witch. The exasperating thing about Morgana, from my point of view, is that she is invariably and inseparably joined at the hip to King Arthur, and is often described as his half-sister.

Trust me, King Arthur is another Corryvrekan, up there with Columba. The shortest I can say about *him* is this:

> King Arthur is Welsh.
> King Arthur is Scottish.
> King Arthur is English.
> King Arthur (Arzur) was born in Brittany.
> King Arthur was a Romano-British war-lord.
> King Arthur had very strong links with Italy.
> 'Arthur Pendragon' was an hereditary, initiatic title.
> Arthur, the 'Child, Priest-King and Sacrificed God' is a version of Christ.
> His last battle, Camlann, was in: England, Wales, Scotland, Brittany.

There is a thriving tourist industry around Arthur and Morgana in Brittany today that didn't exist when I first went, but I'm not knocking that. There are a couple of places, as I mentioned earlier, that want to claim Le Fay as their own. Near Tréhorenteuc is the wonderfully named Val Sans Retour. It is here that she is said to have imprisoned unfaithful youths, while high above the valley looms the *Rocher des Faux Amants* (rock of false lovers) where she enticed her prisoners and turned them into stone. She also seems to be linked, indirectly, with priestesses on various sacred islands that I'll talk about soon.

And, er, that's about it.

If I start to say much more about the Arthurian stuff, I know that I'll get sucked into a vortex that will take me into endless medieval realms.

I'd probably become like one of those people who step into Faery for only a night and a day, yet find that decades have passed when they return to the mortal world.

Besides, Ryan the Roofer's magnificent van is pulling up outside our house. Even Arthur, the Once and Future King and his witch-queen half-sister Morgana, would worry if *their* roofs leaked, so I'll quit writing now and get the coffee going for the lads.

Chapter 7

October 31st

I must be the worst gnosticky pagan ever, not to realise it's Halloween. Growing up in a coal-mining town in Northumberland, no-one celebrated it much that I can recall. When I first went to America, in 1974, I was staggered by the depth and range of their engagement with the festival, despite being in the middle of the Bible Belt. I'd never heard of Trick or Treat, and still don't understand it, even though all the kids in our street today, and our many grand-kids, are dressing up as witches and zombies; the shops are full of costumes and masks. That's one American import I don't approve of. And although my wife and I do acknowledge our forebears in our own way, I didn't know until last year that Samhain is *not* pronounced to rhyme with HamTrain, but something like *Soo-win*. That's because I've avoided almost all contact with people who are likely to have uttered the name in the past.

At last, I've got the Magickal Diaries of Kim Seymour and Christine Hartley down from my upper room. I really must look at what they wrote with respect to Morgana le Fay, and hopefully I'll be able to move on. I've written about them at length in both *Dancers to the Gods* and also *Priestess*, so in short I would say that Seymour and Hartley were in direct mind-to-mind contact with beings from other dimensions who had, and have, an evolutionary interest in our humanity. The diaries, written in the late 1930s and early '40s, were private documents never meant for publication. They reveal the pair to have been in touch with a variety of Otherworld beings such as: Kha'm-uast and Ne Nefer Ka Ptah, who were historical characters from the reign of Rameses II; Lord Eldon, who had been Chancellor of England; Cleomenes III, a Spartan King murdered upon a Tau cross, from whose body (legends said) a great dragon crawled; Cheiron, the centaur; Melchisadek of Salem - and others. Their accounts also included what may have been far memories of past lives, as well as details of entry into the realms of the Fae that inspired Seymour's long essay appended in this book.

When Christine gave me the Diaries sometime in 1984, she knew that she didn't have much longer to live. That was not clairvoyance on her part but a simple matter of age: she was 87 and not in perfect health.

I set to work in our rented and haunted house at the bottom of Whitehill, in Bradford on Avon, typing them up. The very absorption of doing so and the mechanical effort, pushed me into another level of consciousness. I almost felt I was part of the rites that I was transcribing. This was 'ambience' at its most effective, I suppose, though I didn't grasp that concept then.

Lest I get too distracted by this, I'll start with the very first entry in which Christine refers to Morgana le Fay. Note that within the texts, Seymour is FPD, and Christine is CCT – her maiden name of Christine Campbell Thomson.

February 3rd, 1938

New Moon 4 days old
Self and CCT
2 Q[ueensborough] T[errace]
Both fit, fine weather.

CCT came full of the idea that she was a witch. It struck her as she came into my room. After I lit the Three Lamps she had difficulty in not going out before I was ready. Immediately we found ourselves in Tintagel. I knew the place, she did not. We were back a very long time, I should say many thousands of years BC. We arrived in a small sailing ship, I got the idea Atlantean. I was in armour, leather, with some silver like metal sewn on in disks. I carried her up the cliff path. She was wet, cold, tired and was wearing a thin green dress. She complained of the cold of my wet armour and lamented the warm sunny south. She was very young, very slight, rather unformed, called herself Morgana le Fey, or the Sea Priestess from Atlantis. I was about thirty, thick set, very strong and a soldier of the sacred clan. It was cold and wet and beastly on that hill top. We did not know what to do and invoked Merlin then he came but not clearly. Suddenly the sun came out, the wind, rain and mist vanished and we got quite hot. I think Merlin used hypnotic suggestion. He gave us a clear picture of Lyonesse before it was drowned, and said we had been brought from Atlantis to teach, and that life after life for Thousands of years we should work together as priest and priestess, trained to work as a functioning pair before Atlantis was destroyed. We should rebel and fight and hate each other at times but in the end fulfil our destiny as priest and priestess – a functioning pair.

He gave us a shadowy glimpse of many lives as servers of the ancient Wisdom which lay before us. Then he told us to look back. And we saw an immense line of many Adepts - high priests and priestesses stretching back into the dim ages, and we now work for them as they worked in the past. The vision was strangely clear and I saw L[ord] E[ldon] among them. Merlin placed his right hand on my neck and on CCT's and drove an immense current of force through me and her. It shook me like a leaf in the wind. And he told me that CCT was far in advance of me as a trained and initiated priestess, but I as a soldier was to look after her. L.E. then took his place and told me that I was free of the world in a way that she was not. She was bound to the world by her karma in a way that I was not. That in the future she would break away often from me, but her initiation at Atlantis would drive her back to serve with me. I have to be patient.

They left after a little time and we both felt splendid.

Time 8.30 to 9.45 pm. CCT out much further than usual but remained fully conscious.

At 10.30 pm after tea I gave CCT a block of stone from the cave under Arthur's castle at Tintagel to hold.

She described the castle accurately, position of the path, towers, the gate. The well and the rooms as they are now.

Then a band of raiding Saxons or Norsemen from ships with a blue banner and horse. Gave a minute description of the methods used to defend the castle. She had not been there and did not know the place at all.

FPD

It's odd to be transcribing this again from Seymour's handwritten pages while Ryan the Roofer is on scaffolding outside my window, looking down and in at me like a mighty king seen in profile. I have to concentrate now and put down CCT's typed page using a similar font...

Report on sitting February 3rd 1938

Left to see what 'came' in an empty room, I kept getting 'Morgan le Fay' hammering at me, so we started on that. A headland with coarse grass, a strong wind, grey skies and the surf beating below but out of sight and rain at intervals. Myself, long black hair and a green dress blowing around me. A cromlech...a little footbridge joining the headland to the mainland and a cliff path up the mainland to the bridge past the Cave where Merlin sat. I was cross and bored...hating the place and wanting to do magic but unable to begin before Merlin came. The sun came out for a few moments, a very watery sun and a very few moments and I thought of the Cornish Riviera posters and jeered. Then we talked and remembered how we had come in a little ship from Atlantis, carried forward on one enormous green roller after another, and you reminded me how you had to carry me up the last of the cliff path – and how cross I was. And then

Merlin came and I went into a queer state and there were questions and answers of which I remember very little now except that 'they' must not have much to work with yet because they might recognise me for who I am. I have a pretty strong idea of myself, of who I am, but they don't know it yet. Then I came back and was very tired for a little while. I remember L.E. and Merlin behind me and the feeling of being at the end of a very long line of very important people and of somehow 'mattering' but not knowing quite how.

CCT

There are a few more references to Morgan le Fay in later workings, describing her leaving the great temple in Atlantis just ahead of the cataclysm. Then a brief entry on January 16th, 1939, which concluded:

Later on, we worked again and I picked up Merlin and a cove on the West Coast. And as usual it was beastly cold and wet and I was cross, and the fire wouldn't burn. And then M. came out of the cave and walked over to where we were by the fire and said various things I can't quite remember but chiefly, 'Take care of my Morgan...take care of Morgan le Fay'.

CCT

Thirty years later, when she was 71, Christine told me that she wrote parts of her classic *The Western Mystery Tradition* in a New York hotel room, fully overshadowed by the spirit of FPD. Of Morgan le Fay, she then wrote:

> Of her there is little that we can say, for she is ever the hidden one, the shadowy woman who stands behind, giving of her power from the inner planes. She is the feminine principle of the great Triangle of King, Priest and Priestess; she is the Word, the life-giving Force. She is the Spirit of God, the third person of the Trinity who is or should always be feminine – the Ruach of the Hebrew, the Sophia of Greece, Wisdom that sits upon her seven hills.
>
> Morgan is she who teaches men to work with power; she is Binah on the Tree of Life; the great Mother of form through whom is the manifestation of force.
>
> She is the third of the three shadowy Queens, the old Queen, the Queen-sister of the King, and it is she who takes his head upon her knees in the last journey down to Avalon.
>
> She is also Isis of the Moon, and her place on the Tree of Life can be in Yesod, for in the later pantheon she is changed into Arianrhod. Like all women she is all things and her aspects are infinite. The Church was afraid of Morgan and left her alone; contenting itself with calling her the Witch-woman. But always she draws us back to the primordial sea from which she came, to the old mysteries of

Atlantis, whence our own have derived their life; she is that strange and lovely lady whom we can sometimes glimpse on a rocky seashore, rising out of the water, shadowy in the sea mist and foam. She has all wisdom and all knowledge.[xii]

I wonder if Lua, standing on the shore near Bangor Mór, once had a glimpse of a strange and lovely lady, shadowy in the sea mist and foam, calling to depths within him? I read somewhere that almost all the Celtic missionaries dedicated themselves not only to Jesus but also to that energy they called Our Lady. By this did they mean the Blessed Virgin Mary? or perhaps – in the centuries before the Roman Church turned her into a prostitute – the appealing image of Mary Magdalen? As CCT might have said, the Church was afraid of the Magdalen as much as it was of the Morgana.

It seems that the calumnies heaped upon the latter were the invention of the Cistercian monks who came along 500 years after Lua's time. Influenced by folk memories of the ancient Irish Goddess, The Morrighan (aka Morrígu, Mórríghan, Mór-Ríoghain), this was another triple-aspect divinity representing life & death, sexuality and conflict. From the Morrighan, which means Great Queen or even Phantom Queen, it was a short step to painting The Morgan as black as they could, believing that it was blasphemous for a healer to be neither male nor a member of a religious order.

Remember when you were a teenager and your parents strongly advised/warned you not to go to whatever places in town met their disapproval? For me it was the 'Three Ones Club', a very modest and very sedate dance hall on the edge of town. In my mother's mind this was where 'dorty wimmen' lurked, who were sure to be the ruining of me. Well, I think the tortured monks of Lua's era and long before, created the idea of these islands on which the likes of dark and 'dirty' Morgana lived.

Of course, first chance he got, our Lua sailed off toward the one that was said to be holiest of all, in pagan terms. *Cherchez la femme*, indeed.

But getting back to CCT... In all the times that I spoke to Christine did she ever say: *'Alan, I'm a reincarnation of an Atlantean priestess called Morgana le Fay'*? No she didn't. Not once. Her own present life, extraordinary in itself, was far more important. The stuff that 'came through' with respect to the Sea-Born priestess was probably coming through to others at the same time, particularly Dion Fortune, who wrote the superb novel *The Sea Priestess*, and also perhaps Margaret Lumley-Brown and Maiya Tranchell-Hayes, whom you might want to track down if it bothers you.

I sometimes wonder if energies and entities like Morgana le Fay might best be regarded as Collectives. I certainly think that 'Dion Fortune' herself might be a Collective, because I've met so many people who have linked with her/it on the inner planes and/or have felt that they might have been reincarnations of same. Seymour touches upon something of this, far better than I can, in the appended essay.

How can any reader who does not have the talents of CCT or FPD make links with Morgana le Fay?

Well, I begin to think that the search for, and invocation of, Morgana is a metaphor for the quest toward the highest possible aspect of Love within ourselves and *for* ourselves. And it should be ongoing, ever-becoming. I would argue that you've *all* done so, often. If 'Raasay' has been for me a Time Bud, or Wordsworthian 'Spot in Time', then might not MLF - if I may use that contraction – be a universal equivalent? Just as Raasay as a geographical entity is a complete unknown, yet unfurling all sorts of petals, can MLF have been doing similar for the Western consciousness?

For me her essence is partly evoked in the long poem by Jiddhu Krishnamurti called *Song of the Beloved*, one verse of which runs:

> *In the shadows of the stars,*
> *In the deep tranquillity of dark nights,*
> *In the reflection of the moon on still waters,*
> *In the great silence before the dawn,*
> *Among the whispering of waking trees,*
> *In the cry of the bird at morn,*
> *Amidst the wakening of shadows,*
> *Amidst the sunlit tops of the far mountains,*
> *In the sleepy face of the world,*
> *There thou wilt meet with my Beloved.*

Things are a bit swirly at the moment and I'm struggling for terse metaphors here, but you can probably guess what I mean.

And besides, think... *Think*... Have there been times when you've had oceanic love for someone, projecting all sorts of qualities onto them that you realised, much later, were non-existent? And the person concerned didn't know you felt that way, or had no inclination to return it, muttering the killer phrase 'Let's just be good friends'? In your mind, this person was on a level above you, perfect and powerful, almost unreachable, a reflection of the Moon on still waters. A god or goddess. A male Morgan or female Morgana.

These emotions are all 'sea-born' in a sense – emerging from the great ocean, crawling onto the shore, evolving into whatever is necessary to survive and probably looking really weird as it makes its own way across the beach and into the trees. In a sense these feelings are personal *fata morganas* - something seen from afar that could actually be photographed, yet actually doesn't exist, and which draws you onto rocks.

Is that a bit vague? Here's a mawkish yarn with a twist at the end that might justify a self-indulgence...

I remember on my penultimate trip to Brittany in 1979, I think, I stood at the very tip of the Pointe du Raz, France's equivalent of Land's End, and stared Westward toward a distant, flat and near-featureless island a few miles off shore. Next to me was someone who, at the time, I felt was everything I ever wanted in a woman. She had even indulged me by reading *The Sea Priestess* by Dion Fortune, whose main character is the timeless and mysterious Vivien Le Fay Morgan, a practising initiate of the Hermetic Path who is also a channel for Morgan Le Fay, sea priestess of Atlantis.

Would you be my Morgana le Fay? I asked Jane, standing close by her side, above the jagged rocks and the wild ocean, heart pounding like the waves far below.

Oh... was all she said, moving away with surprise. All the hopes I'd been projecting onto her, and all the imagined futures beyond the immediate horizon of my life, dissolved into nothingness and fell at my feet like sea-spray. Although I didn't know the term *fata morgana* then, she was exactly that.

If you've ever projected feelings onto someone and found, to your dismay and surprise that they weren't mutual, then you've evoked a small version of Morgana le Fay. Ignore those who might sneer and say this is 'only' infatuation: the energies involved are huge and transformative. Any critic who has never felt this should be pitied for their flat lives.

In a sense, the likelihood of Jane becoming my Ultimate Love for All Time was as much a non-reality as Morgana. I mythologised the lass as much as (I am quite sure) Lua and his fellow monks did with Our Lady, and the nuns with Jesus. I don't care how fierce a White Martyr Lua may have been: at some point in his life he would have felt an aspirational surge of Love that he would projected onto a fellow monk or nun. Or if there were no humans in reach among his lonely travels, he would reach toward the Blessed Lady,

Jane and I never became lovers, never even snogged. As I stared that day toward that Western-most isle off the Breton coast, she must have been daydreaming about the fella whose desires she *did* want. We stayed 'just good friends'. She's long dead now, bless her, and I remember her (along with many other souls) on Samhain.

The final twist of this yarn?

When I started writing this book my plan was to research as much as I could about Brittany and its sites, especially sacred isles, including anything I could find about Morgana le Fay's mythic imprint over there. I had fuzzy memories from my reading of one island in particular that had a conclave of nine virgin druid priestesses called the Gallizenae. They were said to be able to predict the future, calm winds, heal, wounds and diseases, and take the forms of different animals. How could I *not* be attracted to a place like that? When I finally tracked down the original reference, from Pomponius Mela, in his *De Situ Orbis*, I was somewhat surprised to find that this was the Île de Sein that I had been staring at all those years ago.

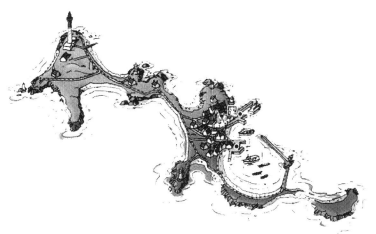

A thousand years after Pomponius Mela, the very idea of such women on such islands was still so powerful that Geoffrey of Monmouth in his *Life Of Merlin* gave new spirit to it by describing the Insula Pomorum, or Isle of Apples:

> There, nine sisters rule...She who is chief among them is the most skilled of healers, excelling her sisters in beauty. Her

name is Morgan, and she knows the properties of herbs to cure the sick.

Modern scholars argue that the women described on the Île de Sein was one of the prime sources for Geoffrey's writings.

Perhaps – just perhaps – unbeknownst to my conscious mind, the Île de Sein was communing with me as I stood on the Pointe du Raz looking Westward, just as much as Raasay has been.

As I've been learning, there really were a lot of such priestess-inhabiting islands around two thousand years ago, either off-shore or in lakes. On the levels of dream and wish, who *wouldn't* be attracted to the very idea of an island where you can get healed, a place of bird-song and beauty and enchantment.

I don't know why they all have to be virgins though.

Chapter 8

November 1st

Considering that last night was the night when the spirits of the dead come closer to us, I didn't have any visitations from either Lua or Morgana, or any of their spiritual cohorts.

Mind you I did have an odd dream in which I was at the coast and was swept away by terrific tides. When I finally got back to town I was unable to remember how I'd escaped – after all, among my many non-accomplishments, I can't swim. After being ignored, a stranger appeared and told me that I was actually dead, and was now an earthbound spirit.

Perhaps I am! Perhaps I died in a bus crash after visiting the Samye-Ling Monastery, and I'm writing all this on an astral laptop in what the venerable Abbot Akong Tulku Rinpoche would call the Bardo Plane. This is a Tibetan concept of course, and refers to an in-between state after death.

Has my whole life since then just been a self-created illusion? Is the scaffolding outside our house nothing more than a mental construct, and is Ryan the Roofer actually one of the trickster spirits said to haunt and taunt on this plane?

Nah…

I got up early and looked on-line at the Raasay Community Newsletter again. I sometimes feel like a peeping tom doing this, even though the issues are all old and no-one on the island wants to take on the newsletter today. If I lived there I certainly would, though I'm not sure they'd enjoy my style. There's just a lovely, simple atmosphere about this realm and I feel a soothing – an ambience - just peeking into it.

Four years from last night, on Halloween, the splendidly named Artemis Panna wrote a brief piece:

> On Saturday October 30, the community stepped out in style to welcome Halloween and the launch of the Raasay While We Wait whisky, courtesy of our local R & B Distillers. The celebrations kicked off at Borodale House with pupils from the primary school leading a torch-lit procession that wound its way down to Clachan beach. Joining them was architect Olli Blair who defied the windy weather to carry an enormous willow sculpture of a Kelpie which was burned on the bonfire. After admiring the flames everyone gathered in the Boathouse to enjoy live music from TROSG and of course, the bar! Much whisky was consumed and the night raised

over £600 which will go towards repairing the Boathouse in time to begin our winter skiffbuilding project.

It included a photograph of a very huge effigy of a Kelpie about to consumed by flames.

I'm coming to love that isle. I'd drink the speciality Raasay Whisky and act stupid at their dances, known as Ceilidhs, where my foot-work during 'Strip the Willow' and the 'Dashing White Sergeant' would be dazzling. Then I'd lead them all singing around the bonfire while the Kelpie sizzled and crumbled, and stagger across to help them with their Boathouse, like that scene in the movie *Witness*, where they all build a barn while drinking lemonade and seething with unexpressed sexual tensions.

Mind you, they do know how to deal with their demons on Raasay – burning the Kelpie effigy like that. We've all got demons of our own, and you should write them down, illustrate them, brood all over the screed and then burn what you have done, watching the smoke disperse into nothingness in the skies. This is not a witchy means of dealing with your enemies and hoping they get blasted. It's a question of being ruthless with your own quirks and foibles, the things within yourself that can cause you to shudder when you glimpse them, usually in the Lake of the Woman that's akin to the amniotic sac in which you formed. It won't create an immediate exorcism of your torments, of course, but it will send a signal inward and upward that you are doing Work within yourself.

November 2nd

If I'm the worst gnosticky pagan of all time, I must rank pretty high in the list of useless seers: England 12 - 32 Republic of South Africa.

'Nuff said.

And the birds in our garden, from under our eaves, have shown no interest in the Monas Hieroglyphical feeders. We're not sure why. After all, there's thrice as many perches so they won't have to fight. I'm sure there's a deep metaphor here, but at the moment I can't see it. Maybe it's because our neighbour's horrible cat, that we call Schroedinger, has seen it too and lurks underneath fancying his chances. Or maybe our little sparrows really are 'bird brains' and can't quite figure out that we've moved the original source.

I'm pretty certain now, that apart from the Valley of No Return in Brittany and perhaps the Île de Sein, Morgana le Fay has no tangible 'place' that we can call her own. I've used Google Earth to scour all over the Île but it seems pretty uninspiring. Apparently there were two megaliths there centuries ago, but not now. And I've since found some speculation that Pomponius Mela *might* have writing about the Scilly Isles. I suppose the sacred isle's location is as controversial as that of Camelot, or Avalon, or Arthur's and Merlin's graves.

It could be that Morgan's true 'form' is a distant ripple from a splash in the aethers caused by a Native British goddess. There was a Celtic Mother-Goddess known as Modron who was often depicted in Romano-British times as having a triple personality. In the Arthurian tales MLF is associated with the Queens of Northgalis (North Wales) and the Wastelands, while the Lady of the Lake may be another aspect. Some early sources actually refer to Morgan as 'The Goddess', with powers of shape-shifting and healing. And to this day, the Breton name for a water-nymph is, apparently, a 'Morgan'.

So...

Am I dismissing the very idea of CCT's 'Atlantean' priestess with the initiatic title of Morgana? No. In the Quantum multi-verse where everything that can happen does happen, the Atlantean stuff is an entirely potent approach. I was going to say potent 'myth' but then it might seem that I was diminishing the reality. Our own lives are all myths, and are entirely real. And I do think that there are energies and swirling currents of Old Magick there that can be Worked, but at the moment she feels very distant.

I'm wondering whether I need to go to Brittany next year at all.

Now that Ryan the Roofer has fixed our tiles and removed his scaffolding, we're in search of the equally elusive Dave the Door Man to stop the huge Westerly wind from whistling through our kitchen. I've done everything a man can with lashings of mastic stuffed into the cracks, but the cold Air still bites. Years ago Paul Brunton wrote the influential and best-selling *A Search in Secret Egypt* and *A Search in Secret India*, detailing his adventures with various sages. I should write *A Search in Secret Wiltshire* about my unending quest for sage people who can actually fix things, with talents that are as wondrous to me as the Indian Rope Trick. I know that magicians bang on about the Cup, Rod, Sword and Shield (Water, Fire, Air and Earth) and use these in their Rites of Light, but – as someone who is famously inept at DIY - I'd prefer someone to do it for me.

When I was talking the other day about exorcising demons, as inspired by the burning of the Kelpie on Raasay, it got me musing…

I don't doubt that throughout human existence there have been other-world and inner-world entities that have clashed with us. Perhaps they were fundamentally hostile toward us because they saw *us* as 'evil'; or perhaps they were just out of alignment, and needed tolerance. Joan Grant [1907-89], described an encounter with an inner-plane creature near Aviemore, in the Scottish Highlands, where she had been bathing next to a burn. She described it as '…utterly malign, four-legged and yet obscenely human, invisible and yet solid enough for me to hear the pounding of its hooves.' [xiii] She ran for her life to escape from what sounds very much like a Kelpie.

And there is the famous story of St Columba who challenged a 'monster' in the River Ness that was about to attack one of his followers. As the beast approached Columba made the sign of the cross and said simply: 'Go no further. Do not touch the man. Go back at once.' The creature stopped as if it had been pulled back by ropes. Columba's men and the accompanying Picts then gave thanks for what they perceived as a miracle.

I'm guessing that the Wild Places of the world were once filled with them, but I'm wondering if perhaps they are no longer so numerous because, over the centuries, the likes of Moluagh and Columba sent them 'on'?

There is a cheeky but important story about the curmudgeonly magus Bill Gray. Sometime in the 1970s he was called to a farmhouse near Cheltenham to deal with a particularly troublesome haunting. He did his stuff and the house returned to its former calm. However, unbeknownst to him, the house next door suddenly experienced all the same manifestations. Then it was the somewhat non-human, utterly beautiful and uncanny Murry Hope, using a differing sort of magick, who finally put the noisome spirits to rest, instead of just blasting them across the fields.

Kelpies and other such creatures are very real on the inner planes. But maybe, over the centuries, they have been encouraged, like St Columba's monster, to 'Go back at once.' You only need to read the on-line magazine

Nexus to see that Bigfoots and similar are busting out all over. While I might doubt the physical reality of these, I feel sure that they are a Kelpie-like presence on the inner planes. And they don't necessarily want to bond with us.

I'm suddenly thinking of that malign and non-human beast we call Schroedinger. Despite me saying in ringing tones 'Go no further. Do not touch the birds. Go back at once!' it just ignores me, or else doesn't understand simple English. Margaret has put some holly and spiky twigs in the area where it lurks and likes to crap. Maybe Bill Gray laid the psychic equivalent in that house he exorcised.

November 11th

I might forget about Samhain, but I'd never forget the 11th hour of the 11th day of the 11th month. This is when the Dead enter my head in great numbers, and I have a minute of silence to remember all those who gave their lives in all the wars, on all sides. I like to think that I'd have been a brave and good soldier but I doubt it, and was never put the test anyway.

So I spend a moment having a good Think and a sad Remember of the people lost to wars in my own family, and watch as the sparrows go back *en masse* to the original, single feeder that we resurrected: it was clear they distrusted the Monas Hieroglyphical one. They're rioting out there at the moment. I'm not sure what I can learn from this mini war in heaven, or the secret dealings that should be teaching me things.

I was not too surprised when Raasay nudged me.

I saw in their Newsletter that four years ago, on the eleventh hour of the eleventh day of November, Rosemary Bungard led a short service of remembrance for all faiths at the war memorial at Suisnish. Raasay folk of all denominations attended the service which ended with a rendering of the verse 'They shall not grow old' by ex-serviceman John Thomson.

The basic details of losses from Raasay and neighbouring Rona from the War Memorials Register are rather heart-stopping:

First World War (1914-1918)
Total names on memorial: 22
Served and returned: 0
Died: 22
Exact count: yes

Second World War (1939-1945)
Total names on memorial: 6
Served and returned: 0
Died: 6
Exact count: yes

It will do me no harm to look out over my garden now and quietly read out their names, as they appear on the obelisk overlooking Churchton Bay. It's the least I can do for them at the moment, even though they don't know I exist. I read a lot these days about people having unseen psychic 'attachments' that can drain their energies. I wonder if I'm becoming something of an 'attachment' to the collective psyche of Raasay itself.

Goodness know what the population of those two islands was in 1914 but those 22 soldiers must have comprised the bulk of the fighting-age males. Were they all conscripted? From the little I had read about Raasay's history, it seemed that Kings and the aristocracy, not to mention their own Clan Chiefs who were often short of money, had not always dealt kindly with the awkward occupants of the isle.

The people of Raasay supported Bonnie Prince Charlie in the 1745 Rising and sent soldiers to his cause, including 23 pipers. Although the clansmen fought bravely the 5,000 Highland soldiers were no match for the 9,000 soldiers of the brutal Duke of Cumberland, at the fateful battle of Culloden in 1746. All but 14 of the Raasay men returned home but it was a turning point in Scottish history and hopes. From then on…

- The wearing of Highland Dress or use of tartan was prohibited.
- Bagpipes were forbidden to be carried or even played.
- Catholics were debarred from holding any pubic office and were unable to move freely through the country.
- The Episcopal Church was severely restricted and could have no more than six worshippers.
- Those Highlanders and Islanders who could not read or understand the new Disarming Act had to agree to its rules by swearing an oath on their dirks.
- Anyone breaching the Act would be sentenced to six months imprisonment or transportation to 'Plantations beyond the Seas'.

To punish the people of Raasay for supporting the Pretender, the Hanoverian government in London sent soldiers with orders to destroy everything. They killed all animals in their path, not for food but for revenge, leaving the carcasses rotting on the ground. The Jacobite Bishop Robert Forbes was given the news that: 'The whole of Raasay had been plundered and pillaged to the utmost degree of severity, every house and hut being levelled to the ground; and there was not left in the whole island a four footed beast, a hen or a chicken.'

When Bonnie Prince Charlie fled after the battle, a huge reward of £30,000 was offered for his capture. That's equivalent to nearly £4,000,000 today. He was spirited from island to island, including a brief spell in Raasay, before he eventually got to France. Many Highlanders helped him. None of them tried to betray him.

The Highlanders shielding their Prince were every bit as brave as those who, in 1914, went to France to fight for King and Country.

I've spent a long time just brooding on all this.

It's made me hugely sad.

I've no idea what lessons I should be learning.

Chapter 9

November 13th

Very cold today. 8.30am. The birds are going wild at the feeder again. Three big fat pigeons waddle around below, picking up their spills. We call one of them El Chapo. I wonder if our birds have a breakfast time related to the sunrise? I suppose some ornithologist might see this as a stupid question; there is no such thing as a stupid question. There is no sign of Schroedinger.

I woke up much earlier feeling vaguely guilty that I've been neglecting Morgana le Fay. After all, it was my urge to visit her sites in Brittany that prompted this book. Then, when the Raasay time-bud started to unfurl its petals, I seem to have lost sight of her. I wonder if, in some mytho-guilty way, I'm betraying her. You know what I mean… the sort of thing you do in your younger days when you turn all your attentions onto your partner's exceedingly attractive friend. And then you wonder why your partner gets miffed, and you tell him or her not to ask stupid questions.

Sometimes on the edges of sleep, I indulge in a simple fantasy of becoming Lua. I imagine myself standing on a flat stone to sail across the Irish Sea to his first port of call on Lismore, which might mean Great Garden, from *lios* and *mòr*. In my fantasy (it is no more than that) I skirt around Corryvrekan and acknowledge the pods of orca as they curve past, singing their whale-songs, before I arrive at an Eden-like paradise, soaking myself in a very good ambience.

It struck me last night that if Muirgen/Morgan are titles which mean 'Sea Born', then I can play a simple game by converting this to the English 'Sea Borne'. That is, **carried** by the sea. I had been carried away by the sea in my dream a few nights ago, so I was briefly a Morgan. And Lua had certainly been borne by the sea as he set about converting the Western Isles. In a way that might have horrified the lad, Lua was also something of a Morgan.

I've not been able to find out much about Lismore, except that it seems to be a pleasant, mild and fertile isle on which to live today, with a population even smaller than Raasay's. Nevertheless it has a shop, post office, public hall, available bike-hire (there is no petrol sold on on the isle), **two** libraries and what seems to be an excellent café within the Heritage Centre. Lua would think me very shallow for saying this, but when it comes to visiting his ancient sites or spending time in a café then the latter will win every time. I think it was Archimedes who said something to the effect of: 'Give me a lever and a place to stand and I will move the world.' Well, give me a café and a pot of tea and *I'll* explore the universe. That might sound crass, but it's important to me; it makes things work.

The islanders are obviously immensely proud that their small isle (even smaller than Raasay) is both tranquil and unspoiled, surrounded on all sides by stunning mountain scenery, from Ben Nevis in the north (snow-covered in winter) and the Glencoe hills, round, in a clockwise direction, to Ben Cruachan, the hills of Mull to the south and Morvern to the west.

Yet I don't feel the urge to spy on this place as I've been doing with Raasay.

I have to wonder who and what Lua would have found on Lismore. Nine virgin priestesses? Led by a scary Morrigane? Wild druids? He might have missed the Perpetual Harmonies of Bangor Mór, but the scenery around the isle was a much greater perpetual song. People have nourished themselves all life with this sort of soul-food. There seems to be an inherent sanctity about islands and their inhabitants   exist within a landscape so huge that their souls respond to the whispers of another dimension. He certainly made his name there before he went on to Raasay and other places in the Western Isles. On the few occasions when I have dipped my toes into the pre-history of what is now known as Scotland, I always come across the mysterious (to me) peoples known as the Picts. I'm supposing that it was these he had to convert if he was accomplish his mission.

I think I'm still echoing from the names on the War Memorial and the glimpse into the post-Culloden world. I hope Lua never had to get involved in battles. It seems that Warrior Monks in that era were not unknown. If, as they say, he had a long life, then perhaps he was fortunate to have lived in a time and place where the conflicts were less monstrous. Who would his enemies have been? Who was he trying to convert? Did he have to argue exceedingly hard? Did he impress them with miracles? Did he inspire them by his deeds? Why was the White Martyrdom preferable to staying in Ireland?

I really need to find out about the Picts for whom Lismore was their holy isle...

The Venerable Bede, writing in 731, said that the Picts had come from mainland Europe, presumably Scandinavia, to northern Ireland to ask for land, but the Irish sent them on to Scotland. Hence a myth that the Picts were given Irish wives, on condition that they became matrilineal. But from everything modern I've read, no-one is entirely sure about anything to do with the Picts. The Romans noted that they called themselves 'Kaltis'. When they became Christianised, it was only then that they adopted the Roman term 'Pict', which is apparently Latin for 'painted people'.

According to extensive and recent DNA testing, it seems that they were closely related to the Basques of northern Spain. The Basques, in turn, are thought to be the closest descendants of the Palaeolithic people who established the first settlements in Britain more than 10,000 years ago. People in those far off times travelled far more extensively than might be imagined, and it wasn't all driven by the need to conquer or flee ice ages. Neolithic tools found in Raasay, for example, had their origins in the English Lake District. Faïence beads found at Stonehenge came from Egypt. Amber from the Baltic has been found in mound tombs throughout the British Isles.

The Picts themselves had a tradition that their ancestors came from Scythia. A thousand years before Lua's time, the Scythians controlled large swathes of territory throughout Eurasia, from the Black Sea across Siberia to the borders of China. They then extended further and further Westward, and so came to Scotland. A number of sources insist that Scythians were an energetic but peaceful people.

I'll settle for that, for Lua's sake. I'm really becoming fond of him, and his little glyph is still here in our sitting room, radiating away.

Mind you those north-westerly Picts certainly liked their tattoos. And they painted their bodies blue for battle when they did have to fight. The late Paddy Slade, a hereditary witch who lived near Bath, told me that the blue of the woad was an antiseptic. It seems that their language was not identical with the Celts of Lua's Ireland, and some scholars believe they were not Celts at all.

As for their religion, the best guess is that they were polytheists. Possibly matriarchal. They did some wonderful, unfathomable carvings on standing stones and many of these have survived, including one on Raasay, shown below on the left. And also one known as the Serpent Stone, but from another part of what became known as Scotland.

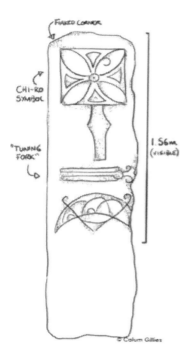

Toby D. Griffen of Southern Illinois University did a lengthy analysis of these symbols as expressed on grave markers. He felt that there was a Cult of the Archer Guardian who protects souls in the Otherworld and seems to protect them from what he can only define as a the Decapitating Beast. He notes that to the Celts the head is the home of the soul, and both the role of the head and its decapitation are also well attested in the Celtic tradition.[xiv] You might want to google the Pictish symbols. I'll put a few below...

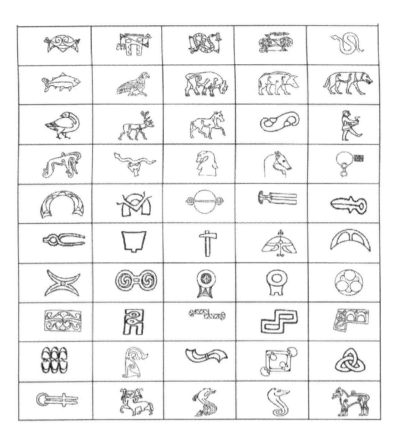

You can see that these are sophisticated glyphs that would have grabbed the attention of Lua and his contemporaries. Try to look at them as he first did. Draw a few. Run your hand over the lines. Try to sense their ambience. Choose one for yourself. Give it an arbitrary name. They would make marvellous and concise, talismanic images, though you'd have to be sure about what energies you were invoking when using them. With all the tattoo parlours around the local towns, and people using symbols not dissimilar to the above, I wonder if the Picts are making their inner presence known today.

I think I'd have liked them. Despite the cult of the head (no worse than the cult of a broken man and the instrument of his torture) I certainly wouldn't want to demonise them and turn them into Huns, as we did to the Germans in the First World War. I hope the people of Raasay after Culloden didn't demonise *all* the English – though I wouldn't blame them if they did.

As for the country we now call Scotland, that was known to the Romans as Caledonia, derived from the Celtic *Caoillaoin*, signifying 'the men of the forest'. Later, Scotland was referred to as *Albann*. In Celtic, *Al* or *Alba* means 'high', whereas *Inn* means 'large island'. The Pictish and later Scottish kings referred to themselves as Kings of Alba up until the Norman usurpation of the Scottish throne after MacBeth.

Living in England, I was taught at school that regular invasions from Angles, Saxons and Jutes during what we then called the Dark Ages, pushed the Native Brits further and further westward. But it now seems that migrations were smaller than usually presented and had an insignificant impact on the nation's gene pool. It used to be argued that the Celts as a whole came from the area of what is now northern Germany, some time in the fourth and fifth centuries BCE, but apparently there is no sign of this in the DNA of modern Britons. Scientists at Sheffield and Oxford found that 99 percent of Britons can trace their origins back to the same gene pool of 10,000 years ago. As for the Irish of Lua's time, Richard Warner, archaeologist at the Ulster Museum commented:

> The image of the Irish as a genetically Celtic people, in fact the whole idea of Celtic ethnicity...is a load of complete cock and bull. The average Irish person probably has more English genes than Celtic.[xv]

It all gets very confusing at this point and I can feel a Corryvreckan swirl coming on. At first I thought that this stuff about the DNA is essentially irrelevant, but I suppose it isn't. Wars have broken out because peoples have imagined themselves as Pure English, Pure Irish or – worst of all – Pure Aryan. If we can begin to see that peoples across the seas, from far-flung lands, are actually just the same as us then we've got a chance of amity and co-operation instead of enmity and conflict. Trouble comes, I think, when some bang on about Sacred Bloodlines., that they often tie up with what they believe is the 'Holy City' of Jerusalem.

If it's any help, Jerusalem is not holy to me. Intrinsically, it is no more holy than *your* local hill, or local river or lake. You can sail away from this sort of tyranny. Perhaps I spent too much time communing with that 'giant' near Skye to think like that now. As far as I'm concerned I'd rather be walking side by side with Wordsworth again through Tintern Abbey, where the magick is more to do with the Land, and where you *feel* you belong – or even where you feel you *should* belong, if circumstances had allowed. This is nothing to do with messianic bloodlines or status or heredity: more to do with the Earth, and the rocks beneath which we can never own, but which can own us.

Which is why, I think, the mountains and valley and lakes of Wales have such a powerful attraction for me and my wife. It's not because we have ancient Brythonic DNA seething below our consciousness, but because something within the Land seemed to speak to us. That must sound pretentious, but it's the best we can explain it.

If we don't get to Brittany next year, we will very definitely make that trip to the Pistyll Rhaeadr waterfall and also nearby St Melangell's Church with an atmosphere that various mystics and magicians whom I respect have almost drooled over.

Melangell, I should explain briefly, was a female saint of the 7th century. She came to the Berwyn Mountains from Ireland and lived as a hermit in the valley. One day Brochwel, Prince of Powys, was hunting and pursued a hare which took refuge under Melangell's cloak. The Prince's hounds fled, and he was moved by her courage and sanctity. He gave her the valley as a place of sanctuary, and Melangell became Abbess of a small religious community. After her death her memory continued to be honoured, and Pennant Melangell has been a place of pilgrimage for many centuries. Melangell remains the patron saint of hares, but above and beyond that seems to be a version of Ostara, the spring goddess.

I like to think that she and Lua would have got on very well.

I won't now worry about Lua's time among the Picts. It's not as if he was making contact with a completely alien culture. English/Irish/Scottish/Welsh/Breton/Celts/Picts – they're all just names, not diagnoses.

I feel I'm babbling. I'll stop now.

November 14th

Margaret is in Brussels at the moment and I'm waiting for Beau the Builder to come. I only hope he doesn't arrive at the same time as Dave the Door Man, as I'll go into meltdown. We've summoned Beau to fix the shed that was damaged by those gales (Air) and also try to figure out why the light doesn't work on our cooker (Fire). Oh – and to damp-proof the outside walls of our bathroom (Water). Not sure I want to find an Earth problem.

Beau is the partner of our fourth daughter Lara Fay. They live together on a splendid barge that he built himself, which is moored in Brassknocker Bottom. Sometimes, they have glimpses of a Green Man peering through their portholes. I pointed out that the little-known-about 'Spring of the Green Man' trickles down from Conkwell on one of the surrounding hills. They plan to get married officially and legally in a Register Office, but have asked me to conduct a separate, magickal ceremony before that. Of course, this makes me hugely proud, and will enable me to evoke my inner priest. I know he's in there somewhere.

He will be magnificent.

November 15th

I should have been meeting a friend of mine at the Archangel in Frome today, but I'm a bit fluey so I called it off. It's a rambling, pleasantly shabby, un-posh hotel in the town centre, with various cozy corners. They also have logs for the big fireplaces in winter and I could watch these burn all day. We do the same with the small chiminea in our garden, just sitting watching the flames in silence. I think that's a human delight that everyone has, and must be an ancestral thing going right back to the various Stone Ages.

I got a Facebook message last night from a young woman who mentioned, apropos of nothing, her fascination for the mystick isle of Hy Brasil. Pity I can't direct Lua or Morgana in that direction because it's a fascinating story, that actually has more substance to it than Atlantis. This mysterious island is said to re-appear off the coast of Eire every seven years. It takes its name from *Breasal*, the High King of the World, in Celtic history. He may or may not be related to *Bresal Echarlam mac Echach Baethlaim*, from the stories of Lugh at Tara, that I might have to mention soon. He was *not* St. Breasal, although pre-Christian folklore about Hy Brasil may be the foundation for that saint's legends. I like the thought of the 'High King of the World'. Perhaps I'll write a novel one day about King Breasal leaving his sinking land as Morgana le Fay was said to have done. I'll make sure he keeps well away from GlasVegasbury though.

I've often thought that myth and legend act like water on the earth: they keep it moist and fertile, and can hydrate us on inner levels. That might sound a bit far-fetched but consider this and – most important - find your *own* parallels...

When I was 14, on a school trip, we were all thrilled to be taken around the legendary Sherwood Forest, quite some distance from our town in the north-east of England. Even though we were savvy enough, even in those innocent days, to know that Robin Hood never existed, it was still so exciting to be there, in the greenwood – *the* greenwood!

When I was 44 and they filmed *Robin Hood, Prince of Thieves* in various locations here in the far-away south west, there was a little boy in me that still got a frisson – a sense of ambience again – by being at these sites, where Robin Hood had flirted with Marion.

Now that I'm 68 I have light-hearted internal monologues about who was the best Robin Hood: Richard Greene, Errol Flynn, Kevin Costner, Sean Connery, Russell Crowe Patrick Bergin – and a host of others. Of them all, Costner is the man for me. But if it came to a *real* fight, then you'd want Errol on your side every time.

What I'm saying is, during this fluey moment, that the Land can be made moist with myths, and that you can feel this. There was no actual Robin of Locksley as we might visualise him, any more than there was a Morgana le Fay, but when you connect him with the Land then you can almost hear the twanging of his great bow.

Again, bear with me if I seem to be veering toward crassness. In C.R.F. Seymour's long essay that I append to this book, you'll see all sorts of similar ways in which you can slip into the Otherworld and – who knows – find you own Heroes and your own inner Greenwood.

I'm wondering now, as I wait for the postie to come, if Lua had any sense of where he came from. I mean that in two senses: physically, in terms of where he was born and raised; spiritually in terms of his Christianity and all those magickal and mythological currents that swept over the landscape of Ireland before St Patrick arrived and tried to kill them off, like snakes. Patrick died in either 461 or 493, depending on which annalist you choose, so Lua wouldn't have known him.

You see if our lad had - literally – turned his back on Bangor Mór and stared inland then he would have been looking Westward toward the great pagan Ulster capital of Eamhain Macha, where for centuries they knew all about the likes of Morrigans and Triple Goddesses. Perhaps the very essence of Morgana le Fay might ultimately hail from there. If Lua was Irish born and bred, then he would have been brought up in the ripples from Eamhain Macha. He might have absorbed their ambience as I once did in the greenwood of Nottinghamshire.

It's well known now that the Roman Church built upon existing sites of ancient worship in their attempt to wean the pagans away from their traditions. Indeed, St Patrick founded his principal church in Ireland at nearby Armagh, that place ever since maintaining the grand title of 'Primatial City'.

Eamhain Macha is central to the grouping of stories known as the Ulster Cycle. These are set in the first century CE, and largely revolve around the legendary figure of Cuchulainn, a warrior in the reign of the Ulster king Conor Mac Nessa. It was occupied from the third millennium BCE and so its history spans nearly five thousand years. *Macha* is an important name that has been used by historical individuals, but at the deepest level she is a powerful spiritual entity. The 8th Century *O'Mulconry's Glossary* says that Macha is 'one of the three morrigna'.

Morrígan or *Morrígu*, remember, is the Old Irish name of an ancient war-goddess. The first part is cognate with the Old English *maere*, a word which has survived into Modern English as part of 'nightmare'. The second part, *rígan*, is Old Irish for 'queen'. The word is sometimes used as a generic term for a group of three war goddesses, along with Macha and Bodb. Heads cut off in battle were called 'Macha's Acorns' and one of the chambers at Eamhain Macha was used as a storehouse for the display of enemies' heads. The religion of Macha's people seems to have been a warrior cult of war and death. Gods and Ancestors, War and Slaughter. Apparently at the height of the Troubles in what is now Northern Ireland, this specific area was known as Bandit Country.

Dr Richard Warner has argued that Navan, to give the modern name of Eamhain Macha, was made to be a conduit between this world and the Otherworld, a portal to the homes of the ancestral gods. He felt that the mound was made as a platform on which druids would perform ceremonies and on which kings would be crowned, while drawing power and authority from the gods and ancestors. Navan was thus an Otherworld place, the home of the gods and goddesses. It was a Celtic tribe's sanctuary, its capitol, its sacred symbol of sovereignty and cohesion.

Much as I loathe 'Rome', I begin to see why Patrick's relatively simple message might have appealed to the ordinary folk. Anthony Duncan, an extraordinarily fey priest within the Chruch of England, identified an almost demonic element in Celtic paganism, adding: 'A religion of propitiation is in any event a religion of fear, of psychic dread, and it may be of significance that there was no Celtic goddess of love.'[xvi]

And I'll bet Lua's mum would have urged him to keep away from any remnants of Macha's lot. If that sounds crass, just remember that before he became 'The Clear and Brilliant, The Sun of Lismore in Alba', he was his mother's little boy, and she would worry herself sick about his every cold and fever, and would be willing to die for her babby, or kill in order to protect him. That's certainly what I felt about my babies as they arrived. If you've never felt that your own parents were like Lua's, then I'll bet there is a sense of damage or bewilderment within you.

We really don't do such people favours by labelling them as holy Saints or mighty Adepts and seeing them as gleaming islands in the ocean of humanity. They are the same as us. They have to be reachable.

I'll have to have a Good Think about the true nature of Celtic Christianity before too long because I have various inner torments that I'll share in due course. As for Morgana and Brittany, I feel at the moment that I'm looking at through the wrong end of my inner telescope. Perhaps, like Hy Brasil, they will pop up again from the mists when I least expect.

Margaret's train back home is delayed. A suicide on the line between Trowbridge and Westbury. I'll stuff myself full of paracetamol and go and get her.

Chapter 10

18th November

Didn't sleep well last night. A bit feverish, I went into the spare room so as not to trouble Margaret. This is now habitable and the ceiling no longer drips, thanks to Ryan the Roofer. The sky was very bright, though I could see nothing out the rear window. I'd hoped to glimpse either a hovering UFO or the Leonid meteor shower, but it was just a clear sky and a few stars. Perhaps the moon was shining around the front of the house. Still no sign of Dave the Door Man, and Beau the Builder is ill.

I note that in Kim Seymour's Diaries he almost always gives the phase of the Moon, as he clearly felt his rites were influenced by it. Perhaps I should be doing this. I've just googled and found that last night it was in a 'Waning Gibbous Phase'. To my shame, this means nothing to me. The next Full Moon will be on the 26th November, and it seems to be given the name of the Mourning Moon. (That will be the day after St Katherine's Day, named after a non-existent Christian martyr who was actually a local and near-forgotten pagan goddess of the West Wiltshire area.)[xvii]

The late Dr Arthur Guirdham [1905–1992] noted once that a matron with long experience of working with the mentally ill swore by the unsettling powers of the Full Moon upon her patients. Guirdham's books, contentious though they are and out of favour, had an enormous impact on me, but I've never fancied myself as one of his reincarnated Cathars or Celtic Christians. Although he lived across the fields from me when I was on Winsley Hill, and we communicated by writing when I lived In Bath, I never met him. For me, below and beyond his yarns of group reincarnation, he inspired a sense of the Spirit of Place that has never left me, and the simpleness of the Dualist outlook. Although I was somewhat in awe of the man's intellect and insight, I immediately disagreed with the matron he was quoting. I have had *long* experience of working with the mentally ill at the very sharp end – adults and children – residential and in the community – and in all the days and nights I worked I never once felt that the disturbances were lunar inspired. A high wind would get individuals troubled – but never the Moon.

But you can imagine the sheer power and beauty of a Full Moon during Lua's time when the whole world was what would now be classified as a

Dark Sky zone. Years ago Margaret and I went to the Avenue at Avebury to watch the rise of a Super Moon and we were somewhat startled by the speed with which it rose from behind the hills and seemed to fizz across the heavens. If the stones were ever alive, they were that night. I suppose, looking back, we were both in a delightful state of madness just standing there watching it soar. We wanted to sing but didn't, as there were others around, and must have just stood there with lunatic looks on our faces.

So maybe the matron was right after all.

This morning, outside one of the cafés in town, two young men had some placards up, offering to explain why the world is in such a mess. They were cordial, cheery, well-dressed and not at all pushy. I took one of the leaflets and promised to read it, but walked on. I'm not being scornful here. In fact I've got enormous respect for all such people who walk the talk. When I was young I never dared to publicly spout about the things *I* believed in: I feared being sucked into a vortexof scorn.

But as I saw them I was reminded of the two modern stained-glass images of St Moluag. It was as though these slid across my brow's cinema screen, and it made me realise something... Dear Lua is not alone in either image. There is a young man standing behind him in both. Remember that legend I mentioned earlier? There was a bet between him and St Mulhac that the first one to land on the isle of Lismore would have the right to found a monastery there. Moluag cut off his finger and threw it ashore in order to claim victory.

I think that Lua inspired the artists to try and tell us something...

I am glad he had some support during his mission. Whether this young man was a biological brother, a Brother in Christ, a follower, novice or a lover, isn't important.

It has made my thoughts flow into a yarn about Arthur Koestler, so I'll have to go with them. Koestler was a heavy-duty philosopher who, after a diagnosis of terminal leukaemia, committed suicide with his wife at their home in London in 1983. In his last years he was approached by a young man who wanted the answers to life and all its messy torments. Koestler told him that there were only two important things:

- First, be connected; whether to a person, place or even an object, doesn't matter.
- Second, it is more important to love than be loved.

That, as far as Koestler was concerned was the very essence. And despite all those things that leaped out of the book at me in the Samye Ling Monastery fifty years ago, and all the millions of words I've read and probably written in the years before and after that moment, those two bullet points sum up everything for me today. Y'see the excitements I felt at learning about First Orders, Third Orders, Hermetic Orders, Adepts and Sun Masters and Secret Chiefs; the Stella Matutina, Golden Dawn, Amoun Temple, Cromlech Temple... all these and a million ripples more are far less important than simple human connection with my habitat and my fellow man, however awkward I might find the latter at times.

I'd like to think that Lua and Mulhac took something of this attitude with them to Lismore. They certainly wouldn't have had leaflets to give out. How on earth did they win over the apparently fierce Picts? How did they communicate? - was there a kind of *lingua franca* being muttered around the Highlands and Islands?

How would those two men outside the cafe have converted *me*, or at least just got me to listen carefully to their message? Through kindness, humour, honesty and presenting themselves in such a way that – over and above whatever their leaflet might say – I could look at them and say to myself: *I want to be like them*. I think that was the Celtic Christian approach.

Or perhaps Lua himself was seen as something of a wonder-worker, and could heal. There *are* such people you know! And I think more so then, in the 6th Century, when there would have been less resistance to such notions and talents. Or perhaps, if he really was connected with Irish royalty, then he made diplomatic use of this.

I know I keep saying it but soon, I'll really have to look a bit more closely at this notion of Celtic Christianity...

I'm so fluey at the moment that my mind bobs up and down with its fevers. When I'm 'high' I write this; when the fever hits I curl up and sink. I suppose I should call upon one of the saints whom I writing about at the moment, but I'm not sure they'd come if I called, and I think I'm a bit frightened to put them to the test. 1100 years after he died, folk would go to the church of St Moluag on Lewis to get healing from their mental problems, especially. A certain Captain Dymes visited in 1630 also noted that people who couldn't make the trip 'were wont to cut out the portion of their lame arms or legs in wood with the form of their sores and wounds therof and send them to the saint where I have seen them lying on the altar of the chapel.'

I think I'll stick to paracetamol.

I must confess though, that I'm keen to get Lua to his first port of call at Lismore, simply so I can then move him on to my beloved Raasay, and make more sense of it.

And then perhaps – in a manner of speaking – I'll be able to grab ahold of what Morgana le Fay might have revealed of herself and put her to bed.

I remember that on my first, last and only glimpse of Raasay I assumed that it was a barren and cold landscape. There was also a little bubble of wonder within me that asked why people would want to live on *any* sort of island.

I think we all entertain the notion at some point, even if it's only for a brief stay on a paradise isle for our holidays. For myself, why would *I* want to stay on an island? It's something to do with the encirclement of the sea. Actually I *do* live on an island, only it's massive, and known globally as Great Britain. At regular intervals, like everyone else, I have a deep urge to travel to the seaside. Yet there is an extra urge to find myself completely surrounded by the sea, on an isle that I can circumnavigate on foot. I suddenly remember what I wrote much earlier...

> Morgana means either 'Dweller of the Sea' *or* 'From the shore of the Sea'. Or from the Old Welsh 'Morcant', a

compound name composed of the elements *môr* (sea) and *cant* (circle, completion) or *can* (white, bright).

Perhaps I'm using a bit of sophistry here, but maybe each island is a 'sea circle', within which we unconsciously invoke Morgana le Fay. Or perhaps I should be a bit Jungian and suggest it all harks back to being in the amniotic sac.

November 21st

It's late. We should have gone to Bath to see a Pink Floyd tribute band but I'm still a bit grotty. Gave the tickets to Lara and Beau instead. So I'm browsing the Raasay Newsletters again, and see that for the month of December the island has full programmes of: Football, Yoga, Calligraphy Workshops, First Aid courses, Knitting Bees, Sponsored Walks, Family Dance, and an evening of mulled wine and mince at the community stores. There is even a visiting mobile library, and as an ex-mobile librarian myself this make a noise in my head like the Hallelujah Chorus.

The newsletter also advertises a 'Meditative Walk', leaving from the ferry terminal. 'Join us to enjoy a walk in the beauty, peace and silence of Raasay, visiting some of the island's magical places.' I would go on that one. I wouldn't say a word.

Something of the ambience of the Raasay time-bud soothes me, and compensates for not hearing *Dark Side of the Moon* or *Piper at the Gates of Dawn* last night. Plus I feel the need to fill out my inner glimpses of Raasay with hard information, probably to compensate for the complete lack of this for Morgana le Fay.

As I drove along from Applecross to Plockton all those years ago and first glimpsed Raasay without even knowing its name, I did think that people must have been quite odd or desperate to make landfall on a cold and bleak island and fashion a hard living with a constant battle against climate. I was surprised to learn that several thousand years ago the climate of Raasay was actually pleasant. It was relatively warm and dry with summer temperatures four to five degrees warmer than today. This encouraged settled farming, and there are several recognisable round-house farmsteads to be found on Raasay.

Margaret Moody wrote a short piece in the Newsletter:

The earliest evidence of human occupation on Raasay dates from the Mesolithic (Old Stone Age) period around 8500-4000BC. These early Raasay inhabitants were hunter gatherers and fishermen who lived a nomadic life moving around the island according to the seasons and the availability of food sources. They inhabited caves, rock shelters and tent-like structures made from tree branches and hides. They left behind middens with fragments of bone and nut shells amongst the mollusc shells, marking their places of occupation. Stone tools and knapping debris have also been uncovered at these sites. In 2001 a data report on Scotland's first settlers was carried out under the direction of the *Society of Antiquaries of Scotland*. Raasay's survey was undertaken by three local archaeologists including Martin Wildgoose. Among their finds was an important Mesolithic site at the old pier at Clachan. They found evidence of ancient tree roots embedded in the sand which suggests the bay was tree-covered at that time. There remains much more to discover about the lives of our ancestors on Raasay.

In fact the island also has a number of Neolithic sites (New Stone Age) covering roughly the years *c.* 4000-2500 BCE. The people lived in settled communities working on the land. Burials would appear to have been communal in barrows or chambered tombs. Stone circles or standing stones can be found in sacred or ritual areas. Several sites located between Kennel Wood and Eyre show evidence of at least chambered tombs. Eyre seems to have been a burial area for at least 900 years. Artefacts of this period sometimes found included stone axes, arrowheads and pottery.

I'm often banging on about Names and their meanings. But what is the symbolism behind the very name of Raasay? Of course, as Isle of the Roe Deer it would been given that name because of – I would assume - their prevalence. But what does this actually symbolise? Can we squeeze some meaning from it?

> In Celtic tradition there were two aspects of the deer: the feminine element, called *Eilid* in Gaelic, the female red deer, symbolizing femininity, gentleness and grace. It was believed that the deer called to men from the kingdom of the fairies to free them from the trappings of the earthly world and taking them to the world of magic. Deer often turned into women in such legends in order to avoid being hunted. On the other hand, there was also *Damh*, the masculine element, which was also related to the sacred and to forests, independence, purification and pride.[xviii]

When the seer Achushla said she saw faeries around me, perhaps they were coming from my Inner Raasay. I should have asked her. Margaret tells me that I'm a good listener but am very bad at asking questions.

It has become important for me to learn these things about the island. I would encourage everyone, wherever they live, just to find out basics of local history, preferably as far back as you can go. It's not about dates or battles, so much, as asking *Why*. I think most people reading this will accept that in the realm between lives, they were able to choose the next one: the relationships the lessons, the status, the karmic links – and I would also add *locale*. Wherever you are as you read this, you *chose* to be there – at least for a time.

Chapter 11

November 23ᵗʰ

The fever seems to have gone. It was never very intense. Maybe getting our roof fixed did the trick, somehow. But I had a dream last night which I immediately scribbled down on the note pad next to the bed. I don't get too serious about dreams and would advise everyone to have the same attitude. Probably 97 out of 100 I just throw overboard as jetsam, as I can see exactly where they came from and how useless the fantasies are. Then there is 1 which might present itself as a Big Dream; 1 that seems to express a *very* mundane Parallel Life; and also 1 which makes me think, gently, *hmmm...* The one last night fitted that category. It was very simple. I was watching a documentary. I can't remember if it was on a television or at the cinema, and the terms I'm about to use came exclusively from the dream: I don't know if they have a larger validity.

In the dream I watched an Irish hive-master rescue a struggling Queen Bee from a decayed hive. He placed her in a special 'ladybox', with powerful nourishments, and placed this into a new hive that he had crafted. I was made to understand that when She was strong again, the rest of the hive would join Her.

That's all. I woke with a sense that there was some message there for me, some metaphor or parallel, but I'm not quite sure what. I've often wondered if we're all part of a hive, but that's perhaps a magickal speculation for another day.

I'm scribbling all this down at Trowbridge library. In one of the side-rooms a local choir is practising Carols. The ambience is sublime. Some of the clients I used to work with years ago in the field of Learning Disability saw me and came over. I do think that many of these are faery souls trapped in human form, having decided between lives to give it a go. Often they struggle. Most of them have more Grace than I will ever know.

25th November

Yesterday, I was in that delicious state of liminality made possible by half-dozing in a chair during a cold and rainy Sunday afternoon. As I vaguely peered with hooded lids at the image of Lua on our fireplace, I did that simple daydream of standing on a rock and traversed the Western Isles, watching the whales breach and feeling the sun on my head and the green dark waters below my feet as I balanced my way in the shadow of sea eagles toward any Mystic Isle that might have nine priestesses waiting for me.

I also had an imaginary conversation with him. You see, until then, I

was going to call this book *Raasay – an inner route to everywhere*, and was quite happy with this title. I even worked on the cover and was rather pleased with it. But I wondered if perhaps Lua should be the main focus, rather than the island. The 'conversation' went something like this:

Alan, how would you call me?
Well, I'm not calling you 'Saint'.
*No, how would you **define** me?*
In my Mam's tongue, I think of you as a 'canny lad'.
Then how best do you think of my mission?
None of this ascetic White Martyrdom nonsense. To do with Light and Love, hopefully.
So how did I get about to spread that?
By boat. Everyone travelled by boat in those days, it seems.
*So what **sort** of priest was I?*

I thought of the waves and the Isles and shot out of the chair as soon as the words 'Sea Priest' splashed on me, knowing that this had to be the title, because that's *exactly* what he was. He was a real Sea Priest if ever there as one. I looked back at an earlier chapter in which I was trying to fathom the meaning of his name, which in Scots Gaelic means Pebble, while Irish translates it as Water Praise. Maybe the latter was related to this new notion of him being a *real* Sea Priest. Of course this is both an echo and – some will sneer – a derivation of the title *The Sea Priestess* from Dion Fortune's truly magickal novel about the character Vivien le

Fay Morgan. I can only say that I never saw this coming from Lua, and the more I thought about it the more apt it felt. I don't imagine Dion herself would disapprove of me using it. I'm sure that in her own way she would let me know if she did.

I would add here that the above 'conversation' was not a psychic mind-to-mind communication of the sort that any good medium can have. It was purely a literary construction. I do envy the skills of the Real Ones, as I think of the better magicians, but I've never had any such talents myself. I could yarn until Doomsday about the countless self-styled channellers who have sought to cajole, direct, bully, tempt and awe me by using supposedly mind-to-mind dialogues with exalted Beings. These have varied between being completely wrong, or completely inane. Because I'm not very good at confrontation, I've always replied as carefully as I could: 'Thank you for that, but please tell Ganesh/Sobek/Merlin/Dion/Penry/etc that I'm *not* going to give up my day job and spend my time co-writing books with you.'

Which brings me, I feel, to one of the historical Real Ones, namely Columcille, who was later venerated as St. Columba. A prince of the realm and directly related to the High King, he had all the (well-attested) otherworldly talents you might want in such a figure: royal blood, healing, prophecy, clairvoyance, deep underlying torments and a charisma that oozed out of him like the Star Jelly at Loch na Mna.

In my last job before I retired, I had a manager who always made me think of Columcille. That was my first impression when I met him and shook his huge hand. *Columba*, I thought, though it was a whimsical one. I never imagined that my boss was any kind of reincarnation, or that some Guirdham-esque saga was about unfold. I'd simply been absorbed by Timothy Leary's notion that the universe has innumerable 'scripts' for which we provide the actors. Everyone of you reading this will at some point re-enact one or more of the great mythic scripts. It does not mean you will become avatars or reincarnations of the figures involved, but 'continuations'.

Keith, to give him his name, had no occult powers but he scared me. He was Lord of all the Lorries, big, loud, certain, knowledgable, aggressively direct and seemed to see right through me. Yet he was also enormously loyal and protective, inwardly quite innocent and very often daft. We all adored him. In a speech I gave for him later I stole a line of Irish poetry from somewhere and described him as having 'Hands like shovels and a great big heart'.

And this is how I think of Columcille, who more than anyone else is seen as the founder of the Celtic Church. Under him, on Iona, hymns to the Virgin were composed and sung antiphonally in their timber-built choir and carried across the Celtic realms by monks of huge learning and courage. When it came to their Lady they were not honouring the sad, shrunken woman sobbing at the foot of a cross but focussed on Mary's gift to the world, 'the remaking of the universe in her womb, her conceiving and delivering of the Kingdom of Heaven.'[xix] In the eyes of Columcille and the followers of Iona, Mary was an image of fertility who had made good all manner of things after the Fall, and they sang Her praises right hard and loud.

As I said before, this extraordinary man is something of a Corryvrekan for me. Even as I write this I can feel myself being swirled slowly and inevitably toward some irresistible vortex. So I think it's safer and quicker for this Journal-thingy to talk about the *outward* essentials of the Church he founded...

There was the tonsure for a start. The Roman tonsure involved the shaving of the crown of the head, whereas the Celtic, possibly echoing the Druids, shaved the front of the head, forward of a line from ear to ear.

Then there was the argument about the date of Easter, as the Celtic Church had its own method of determining the 'Paschal Moon' which differed from that of Rome.

A century after Lua's time, during the world-changing Synod of Whitby in 664 (which you might want to google), Bishop Colman of Lindisfarne argued for the importance of the teachings of the apostle John, deriving from the usage of Columba and Iona. He was flattened in his arguments by a snide priest from Hexham named Wilfred, who seemed more Roman than the Pope. Wilfred sneered at Columba and insisted upon the authority of Saint Peter.

In the event the Roman priests won, the Kings converted to the Roman cause and caused their subjects to do the same, and this was the beginning of the end for the Celtic Church within Britain. I'm glad Lua wouldn't have been around to see its decline. I really think the world – and its women - lost something precious. It's only now, as the corrupt, monolithic and paedophiliac Catholic Church is beginning to wonder if it should allow married priests or even – whisper quietly with astonishment – *women* priests, that we're starting to heal again.[xx]

Intriguingly, Anthony Duncan argued against the title of his own book when he said that, really, there was no such as 'Celtic Christianity' or the

Celtic Church, because there never was one, separate or definable in such terms, but that there was a Celtic *spirituality* that may have been different and distinct. For him, the Celt naturally relates his origins to myth rather than history. 'And myth, rightly understood, is a poetic means of expressing a truth which cannot be adequately expressed in any other way. The Celt naturally expresses himself in poetry, while the Anglo-Saxon tends toward expression in essentially earthy flat prose.' The two, he insists, have a vital need for each other.

This is clearly understood today by the Navan Centre which, you'll recall, is on the site of Eamhain Macha, where the original pagan religion was all about War and Head-Hunting, and was the epicentre of the Troubles not too long ago. Their website states:

> Celtic Spirituality is understood by some to be Ireland's 'indigenous' approach to the spiritual! Drawing on Ireland's ancient mythology, Celtic Spirituality brings to life the sacred landscape and our relationship with the natural world. Themes of Celtic Spirituality include:
>
> •Our kinship with the Earth
> •The sacredness of place
> •Awareness of 'Presence'
> •Mythology and 'giftedness'
> •The Otherworld

They offer courses on Celtic Spirituality for groups and Pilgrimage groups, and host annual events focused on the four Celtic seasons of the year. These include a 'Celtic Mindfulness' experience for early Spring (Imbolc), Summer and Winter Solstice events and the Wickerman Gathering at Lughnasadh.

And as a micro-summary of all this we might look at J.D. Mackie's comment in his *History of Scotland:*

> 'The Celtic Church gave love, the Roman Church gave law.' the epigram is as true as most epigrams, though doubtless both churches gave both.'

I'm thinking of Arthur Guirdham with his book *The Lake and the Castle.* This purports to be a story of group reincarnation of Celtic Christians from the Lake District, focussed around Bassenthwaite. Some critics won't accept any of this, but I'm with Anthony Duncan when he notes that Myth is a way of expressing awkward and difficult truths. I accept the *myths* of Guirdham, and I also like his argument that early Christianity spread not via precepts and laws, but through tidal waves of what he termed 'psychic contagion'.

26ᵗʰ November

Am working in the library again. Margaret is at Yoga doing the *padmasana* and *sarvangasana* no doubt. She will meet me here and we'll go on to the 'Silver Screen' at the cinema. This is a weekly occasion for the over-55s to see a (fairly) recent fillum *and* have a cup of tea or coffee for the all-in ridiculous price of £3.75. We're going to watch *Ad Astra* which is about an astronaut who goes into space in search of his lost father, whose experiment threatens the Solar System.

I'm wondering if there's deep personal symbolism involved here. Am I trying to find what Lua might have called *my* 'Heavenly Father'? I don't think so. The torments and failings I've felt with respect to my very earthly Dad were dealt with in my book *Geordie's War*, and I think I did him proud, though I still flog myself as to what a crap son I was. The simple truth is my wife and I both love Science Fiction movies. For me, they're just updated Westerns, and I still muse about the co'boy novel I really must try and craft before I get past it.

I wrote much earlier about King Arthur and the various claims that are made for him and the locations of Camelot and Avalon. Which now brings me hard up against this rocky notion of Jesus. In my book-case I have more books about his reality or otherwise than probably any other topic. So here we go...

- Jesus was the Son of God who died for our Sins.
- Jesus didn't exist, and was a Gnostic myth.
- Jesus didn't exist and was an echo of Tutankhamun.
- Jesus was an Essene, who died on the cross and was buried at Qumran.
- Jesus didn't die on the cross and led the Jewish Revolt in 60 CE.
- Jesus was captured after the Revolt and imprisoned by the Romans at Chester, where he died.
- Jesus was an Egyptian magician and an exorcist.
- Jesus was the last of the pharaohs.
- Jesus was a tantric master whose shakti was Mary Magdalen

- Jesus was married to Mary Magdalen, and had children.
- Jesus is an inner plane Master, alongside Kuthumi and Morya.
- Jesus was an extra-terrestrial.

And that's just off the top of my head.

What do I believe? Apart from my complete refusal to accept the very first bullet point, I can pretty much believe everything and nothing as far as the rest are concerned. Perhaps Lua is in my world now trying to convert me, sailing through the endless oceans of the astral light and mooring himself in our sitting room via that little pyrographic icon. Being

a Gnosticky sort of pagan I can accept that there is an inner level of what some might call Christ Consciousness, but for me it isn't tied in with any Saviour. This is one of the reasons I love the equi-armed Celtic Cross wherein all the elements of everything are bound in perfect balance, as opposed to the dreadful torture of the Calvary cross.

Mind you, I did have an extreme experience some years ago when I was seriously ill in hospital and spontaneously found myself whispering: 'May the White Christ come to me...' Honestly I don't know where I got that from, or what the White Christ might be. I described this in some detail in my book *The Templar Door*, so forgive me for quoting it verbatim here:

> Within seconds I heard the nurse at door of the ward call out: 'The Hospital Chaplain's here! Anyone want to see him?'
>
> I was too crocked to be able to call through the curtains around my bed and say Yes. But then, if he had come, what would I have done? Open a rheumy eye and say: 'Are you the White Christ? Can you heal me?' He'd have thought me mad! Actually, on reflection, I think if I *had* done that, something might have been enabled whether the Chaplain wanted it or not, as he'd have become a conduit of sorts.
>
> Instead the moment passed, but a very short while after that the strangest thing happened. It was as though 'someone' standing to my right gave a Homer Simpson-ish *Doh*! of exasperation at my not acting when I had the chance and decided to step in. It was as though this Being grabbed me by the back of my neck, hauled my soul out of my body and duffed it face down on the bottom of the

mattress as I watched, bashing it up and down as you would to empty an ashtray. And then shoved it back in, with the very clear words: 'In ten minutes your body will start to work normally.'

And so it did. When the doctors came in *en masse* to see whether I should go to the Intensive Care Unit, they were bewildered to see me sitting up quite happily and ready to go home.

Wendy Berg, another of the very few Real Ones, wrote the brilliant and ground-breaking book *Red Tree, White Tree: Faeries and Humans in Partnership*. She reckoned that this experience must have been a faery thing. I've since been told by others who work in the Faery Traditions that some of these shining ones have a belief in a White Christ, while others have none at all. In the Hebrides, however, the Viking raiders and settlers used this as a term of scorn: their god, Thor, was red; their calling the Christ 'White' was rather like calling someone 'yellow': it was an insult.

But, ignoring the Vikings, I like the thought of the 'White Christ', and I hope everyone accepts that this is NOTHING to do with skin colour. To me, if Jesus did exist, he was probably an Egyptian. No, 'White' is to do with the ambience again. Pure and simple. Empty sky and deep blue sea. Peace. Silence. Maybe the 'White Christ' is some Energy or some Being I can only call on in extremis. I'll save all future invocations for my wife and my family and not waste it on myself.

On the other hand, at a lower level of supplication, my fluey symptoms and other aches and pains disappeared after asking for Lua's help that night. Did he step in? Or, given the Gnostic slant that All is One and One is All, was it just me and my inner Moluag getting my mind/body/spirit in sync?

I must light a candle and say Hello to him this evening. And, apropos of nothing, I've learned that the closest equivalent to 'Hello' in Irish is the greeting *Dia duit* (deeya gwit) which means 'God be with you.' And the response to that is *Dia is Muire duit* (deeya iss meera gwit) which means 'God and Mary be with you.'

(We've just come back from seeing seeing *Ad Astra*. We both reckoned on a disappointing score of 5·5 out of 10. I saw no metaphors for my own present life within the story. And the attack of the Space Monkeys rather spoiled it for me.)

I feel that I must let Lua make landfall at Raasay now, and build his chapel there, the remains of which still stand. It's been estimated that he unded 100 such places cross the Isles, although church histories seem to define these as monasteries. I can't think they would have been big places attracting large numbers of lost souls seeking white martyrdom. Still, at this remove of time and place, who knows? With such an itinerary he can't have stayed long on Raasay.

You know how it feels when you discover something unexpected and entirely impressive about someone you've known for years? Well I was surprised to learn that apart from starting his 100 small monasteries across the Highlands and Islands, he founded on Lismore, Rosemarkie and Mortlach, centres of teaching that were effectively universities. It's significant that all three were important enough to become the seats of the Roman Catholic Sees of the Isles, Ross and Aberdeen. They knew a good thing when they saw one.

Further, on another level and era, The Royal House of Lorne, with whom Lua must have had amicable dealings when he arrived on Lismore, became the Kings of Dalriada and eventually united with the Picts to become the Kings of Scots. So Moluag was regarded as patron saint of the Kings of Dalriada, and therefore was highly likely to have been seen, during the so-called Dark Ages, as the first Patron Saint of Scotland.

Even further afield, in the midst of the Irish Sea, he also became the patron saint of Rushen, in the Isle of Man, and (according to Lismore tradition), the whole island. Margaret's distant forebears lived on the Isle of Man, so maybe there's something else going on in this respect.

Because of my love-affair with Raasay I've wanted to think that dear Lua might have ended his days there, but the date and place of death is given as the 25th June 592 at Rosemarkie, in the north-east of Scotland. From what anyone can tell, his body was later returned to Lismore, his first and personal Holy Island, which might have vied with Iona if the currents of history had flowed his way. I can't really say goodbye to him yet because I still feel an amiable, light-hearted and even whimsical connection.

As I write that, it strikes me that this concept of 'whimsy' is as useful as that of 'ambience'. Seeing Keith as Columba is one example. The two evangelists outside the cafe as Moluag and Mulhac, another. I'm sure that 'out there' somewhere are two people being 'continuations' of Seymour and Hartley. Plus there are infinite continuations of the trinity involving Arthur, Guinevere and the great du Lac, and I daresay many of you will have been part of that triangle too.

Be whimsical for a moment, be mythical... Who are *you* a continuation of?

Chapter 12

No sign of Dave the Door Man but the weather is so mild we're not suffering. Beau the Builder will be here next week. They are both ethereal presences in our house because of our needs, but are not physically here yet. I suppose I could say the same about Lua and Morgana. The sparrows in our garden are rioting around the feeders. There is no sign of the cat. Perhaps that time when I echoed Columba's exorcism of the River Ness monster, crying: 'Go no further. Do not touch the birds. Go back at once.' - perhaps it worked after all! Or maybe the sharp, spiky branches Margaret laid in its lurking places was what really did the banishing.

But what about Morgana le Fay? Have I forgotten her? No, but she is very much 'cloud hidden, whereabouts unknown' at the moment. When I visualise the Pointe du Raz these days and look West toward the island where I thought I might find her, I no longer have any frisson of excitement. Also, I found a reference to the Greek historian Strabo, writing in his *Geographica* around 7 CE, who described an island on the River Loire, near Nantes in north-west France that was occupied exclusively by a community of Celtic priestesses. So maybe I was always looking in the wrong place and wrong direction.

I do remember though, in my teens, buying an odd little tome called *The New Dimensions Red Book*. This was not a communist tract, but a selection of articles from the influential New Dimensions magazine. The intention of the editors was to bring out successive books according to the colours of the spectrum, though in the event they never got beyond the Red. Looking back, this was one of the most important books of my life.

For one thing it contained the first photograph I'd ever seen of the mysterious Dion Fortune, whose novel *The Sea Priestess* I first read at a sitting. And there was one essay by Gareth Knight called 'A Guide to Experiments in Astral Magic' that set my nape hairs tingling, plus a very long essay called 'The Old Religion' by the even more mysterious FPD. Many years later Christine gave me the original typescript of that essay, which she called simply 'Kim's Book', as I've already explained.

I've included 'The Old Religion' here as an appendix to *The Sea Priest*, not just as an homage to FPD, but also because it is, without exception, the finest essay on self-initiation into the Celtic Mysteries I've ever read.

But for the moment, let's take a quick peek into Gareth Knight's essay which had an immediate appeal. In fact it immediately set me trying to reach the inner plane Mystic Isle that he described in the group pathworking....

8th June 1965

And looking down, just before us, we see a barge - a long low black barge. One imagines like the one the three mourning queens came in to fetch the dying Arthur. A great tall figure is in it, in purple, and we get into this barge, and he has - strange though it may seem in a deep sea - a long pole, and he is punting us along, as it were, and we glide over the surface of the sea, conscious of the starry sky above us dominated by this huge stellar figure of the planet Saturn, and we approach an island. And the great dark purple figure pulls up the boat before we reach the island, and we are going to remain a little way off shore.

The island is a grey kind of volcanic rock and upon it, dominating it, is a nine-sided building, shaped something like a threepenny piece, only with nine sides. And as we watch it, the whole island and the building upon it begins to glow and become translucent so that we can see inside a glowing bluey purple greyish bright lozenge, and there, seated on a throne is a great female figure -a queen or goddess of the Moon. She has a heavy ponderous build and white pallor of skin one would associate with the Moon. She may well be one of the classical goddesses dedicated to the Moon. And about her are many moon maidens - there do not seem to be any men in attendance upon her...

The island is becoming opaque now, and it has a grey volcanic look, indeed much as the surface of the physical moon has. The boat we are in turns about and the great purple figure ferries us back. Under the cloak one can discern the wings of the archangel of the Sphere of Yesod, Gabriel, archangel of the Annunciation and of visions. He ferries us back beneath the great Saturn display in the sky, to a point in the ocean where we step out on to the water and begin to sink down into the darkening depths, becoming heavier as we go, until we are in complete darkness and our feet touch the ground of the bottom of the ocean.

We proceed back the way that we came. Find ourselves in the grove of weed and submarine life which is the glade where is to be found the great golden Key of this path and the huge lame club-footed man with the crutch, He salutes us as we pass. We are conscious of the great golden Tau making a faint light on our path.

Back in the dark deep indigo, drifting mist or liquid, feeling under our feet the rough sandy surface and about us the fish or larvae of the etheric plane, and now we come to a curtain through which we started originally.

GK

I spent many a night, before sleep, trying to get to that Isle by my own means. The nine-sided temple on an island in the ancient ocean had huge appeal for me. I was fully aware of the kabbalistic symbolism in the narrative and didn't for one moment imagine there might be an earthly equivalent of that place. I didn't glimpse the Moon goddess or the Moon Maidens but, looking back over 50 years, I do think the very efforts I made created powerful currents for my inner voyages that must have carried me along without realising.

It struck me an hour or so ago that there might be more in our Upper Room that might be relevant to Morgana. Everyone has their own awkward embarrassments that they don't like revealing to the world. Mine is a book I wrote that was given (by the publishers) a ridiculous title and cover, both of which make me squirm: *Ancient Magick for a New Age*. I had to go up and look and gingerly at the text for the first time in several decades.

It contained a second tranche of Magical Diaries that CCT and FPD made after leaving the Fraternity of the Inner Light and joining what was probably the Amoun Temple of the Golden Dawn. I say 'probably' because Christine wouldn't tell me that particular secret, and it wasn't until she had died that I thought of all the questions I *could* have asked to winkle it out of her. These documents included the last two hand-written reports of the Workings they were doing. One of seers Seymour refers to was one Paula Trevanion, but whatever Christine told me about her has long since been forgotten.

If I'd been having second thoughts about making an actual visit to Brittany next year, and feeling somewhat guilty, then perhaps Seymour's account of a visit to the legendary Breton city of Ys might compensate. If I had once soaked up energies from Gareth Knight's Moon Temple then maybe I could get the same from Ys. I find Seymour's reports quite compelling and they definitely evoke a particular ambience within me even now.

Ys is believed to be submerged at Douarnenez, in the Finistère department of Brittany. The story of this sunken city has several versions. Surrounded by powerful sea-walls and dykes it was ruled by King Gradlon, who was either a wretched rake or a kindly man, depending on the variant. His witch-magician daughter Dahut secretly entertained her lover within the palace but, when drunk, stole her father's keys and opened the dykes, flooding the city. Gradlon grabbed his daughter and carried her on his steed Morvarc'h [horse of the sea] until he heard the voice of St. Guénolé commanding him to cast aside his demon passenger or he also will be lost. With his heart breaking, Gradlon abandons his daughter and the waters immediately recede, allowing him to reach Quimper safely. Dahut, meanwhile, becomes a 'Morgen', a siren-like mermaid who is often heard calling out to sailors about to be wrecked. (Morvarc'h sounds as if it might have been a Kelpie. Dahut definitely had a Morgana-like tone even before she became one.)

In brief, in the eyes of Seymour and Hartley, Ys was an Atlantean sea-port.

Notes 11/21/40.
1. Invoked the L. of U.

In a dark wet pine wood very boggy underfoot, with bright blue sky beyond the tree tops. Then L.E. appeared, melted back into a Druid, and again into an Atlantean priest.

He showed us a great egg-shaped crystal, pink, standing on a tripod, and told us to go through the crystal, which we did, leaving the three bodies seated on three stones in the wood, and connected with us by a light ray.

We saw Iona, Glastonbury, and then in very vivid green, Eire!

Then we were over Cornwall and Devon and saw a lovely land, where now is the Channel, and over toward Brittany a great city and its port built of immense stone blocks, with truncated pyramids built on stone steps. (I had been to this drowned city once with Paula). We came to the port and saw the curious sailing boats with high prows; went to the square, and into a low truncated pyramid built of very large stones through a pylon-like doorway. We found ourselves in a fair sized hall.

At either end were flights of steps leading up to a stone altar, above which in the East was a great golden sun, and in the West a great silver moon.

In the centre was a tall tripod with hanging chains, holding a blazing brazier. To the south appeared the figure of a priest -standing by an altar on the top of a flight of stone steps. He said the key to all magic is in this hall if you can find it. We each threw a handful of incense into the fire and the whole hall was filled with a sweet smelling smoke. As this cleared away, a big snake like a cobra was gently swaying above its coils. It was silver bellied, with a golden-green back and deep purple spots, and wonderful gold and violet eyes.

C.C.T. stepped behind me, but I knew him to be the serpent that guards the hidden wisdom, and that the serpent is the key to all magical power. So I opened my heart centre and invited him to enter – and slowly I absorbed him into myself, and then I knew that I had within myself the key that unlocks all magical power,

(CCT felt as if she was just an empty crystal shell) and I had within my being the potentiality of the cosmic hierarchy.

I knew that as an initiate of the Serpent of Wisdom I had to share this power with my syzygy. And turning to the priestly adept who gave me this initiation I saw that he, as an adept, was himself his own syzygy. He had polarized the higher and the lower natures, and so was a complete self-polarizing entity.

I thanked him for what he had given me, and then we went to our thrones, mine in the East, CCT in the West, and we stood beside the altars, the three forming the Triangle of Power, with the Master at the apex.

CCT was then told that the Sacred Isle of the West is not on this plane as an actuality, but in the heart of the initiate, and with others we were to search for it and to rouse its power in 'actuality'.

Then back through the crystal into the three waiting bodies. Sounds of gunfire made the last bit rather hurried.

Under the crystal roof we exchanged magnetism from the three higher centres, then built the colouring purple-blue for the head centres, gold for the heart, green for solar, pink the two lower centres.

Very invigorating. **FPD**

'Syzygy' was a common term used in those early years of psychoanalysis. It has been defined as: 'An archetypal pairing of contra-sexual opposites, symbolizing the communication of the conscious and unconscious minds.'

And then his second report, written *exactly* 79 years ago tonight...

Thursday, November 28. 1940

CCT very tired - I was fit. A blitz (mild) was on. Built up her aura which was rather upset. And then picked up the Irish Fairy Folk.

We found ourselves standing on an immense overhang of cliff looking across the Atlantic. Probably it was in Co. Clare. Behind us was a fortress of great stones built into low, thick walls and without cement. I had a sword and round shield. CCT was in a girl's kit - short skirt. There was a sort of roped path down the cliff. CCT went first. I left weapons and followed. Went down to a cove with a spring about 20 feet above high water. CCT was then very dark with a sort of breastplate of golden topazes. Looking out to sea we noticed that the bay was like a horned moon, and looking into the golden glow of the setting sun I saw an island with two peaks at the side and a smaller peak in the centre. It was dark blue in colour. It was the Holy Isle of the West which is only seen at sunset and thus Mael Dun came to us.

Then a crystal canoe sped over the waves and I saw in it CCT (now wearing long golden hair) dressed as a high priestess with a crown of crystal. But CCT saw Merlin in his blue cloak while I saw him in red and gold. On reaching the

103

beach the canoe up-ended and became a huge cobra with CCT under the crystal hood. Then I saw in CCT's hand a green and gold serpent. It wound itself round my forehead in several coils and crushed itself into my brain - this was agony - the serpent then became part of my brain, and I knew that I had once taken initiation in the ancient Snake Cult of Phoenician Eire. It gave one a tremendous surge of power - and both CCT and self were a blaze of light.

Then it faded out slowly, and we returned by another, easier way to the cliff top. I finished strongly elated and full of the life force.

FPD

What I think is truly important, and utterly relevant to me at the moment, is FPD's comment in the working of November 21st:

> *CCT was then told that the Sacred Isle of the West is **not on this plane as an actuality, but in the heart of the initiate**, and with others we were to search for it and to rouse its power in 'actuality'.*

Is that what we've all been doing during this book? Searching for the Sacred Isle of the West in our own hearts?

I suppose for me it's been something to do with this notion of going Into The West. Of course if I got on my broomstick and belted in that direction faster than the sun, and kept going, then I'd cross the Atlantic, cross America and end up crossing the Pacific to find myself on the continent that is often known as the Mystick East. That's an obvious thing, but sometimes (like the rock strata below the Giant's Head or Raasay's geological folds) it's not immediately evident.

Historically, a lot of earlier inhabitants of Raasay, during times of extreme distress known as The Clearances, really did head into the West to find sanctuary and new beginnings in America. This was a dreadful time, historically, that I must research. I don't want to diminish their movement in that direction by making a crass parallel with the constant direction of my inner compass.

So have I found Sacred Isle of the West in my heart? Raasay certainly settled in my own heart – as did Lismore. And I hope the occasional insights into both have sparked something, however subtle, within my readers. Yet I will insist that you can find all this within your own realms.

But first off, I must insist that despite my admiration for Kim Seymour as the finest writer on Magic within the 20th Century, I don't pay much attention to this notion of 'initiates'. You shouldn't feel inferior if you can't claim such a status. When I was very young, I was in awe of the initiates I read about. Books by and about them seemed to leap into my path at the most unexpected times and unlikely places. McGregor Mathers, W.B. Yeats, Dion Fortune, Aleister Crowley, Paul Brunton and a thousand other apparent wonder-workers were my heroes at an age when my peers idolised local footballers or film stars. I was an odd child, certainly, though I mastered ways of hiding my oddities. To me these people and dozens more were all Initiates. In fact the very word 'Initiate' - always with a capital – thrummed within me like a bell. I'd have sold my soul, then, to be able to access the knowledge and experiences that these were supposedly able to achieve on the inner planes. Now that I'm old I can see that whatever powers they might raise treading around their magick circles, whatever Beings they might channel… they were all human, oh so very human, and made just as many cock-ups in their lives – particularly their love lives - as the rest of us.

The very word 'initiate' simply means 'to begin'. So here is the secret that is hiding in plain sight: **You are your *own* Initiate**. The very act of beginning your *own* Work, however simple it might seem, makes you a *true* Initiate.

So Seymour is right: the Sacred Isle that I fancied visiting is not on this plane as an 'actuality' but within me – and within you. And within the watery confines of that Isle you will be able to make contact with those purposive intelligent entities I talked about earlier – be they plants, trees, hills or rocks. By developing your sense of ambience you will transform your everyday realm and learn to navigate the inner tides of life. With a spirit of whimsy you will find that hitherto unexceptional individuals can actually be seen as Heroes. And by finding our about your outer realm you will realise that loving kindness within your community is far more important and world- changing than any cosmic visions. My own 'time bud' or 'spot in time' just happened to be a mysticky sort of Island that somehow called to me over the years. Perhaps yours will be a hill, river, house, tree or an infinite number of other possibilities that will, in time, open to you.

November 30th

I woke this morning just as the central heating started sending its warm Water throughout the radiators of our house. For a little while I just lay there, balanced on the edge of full consciousness, observing my thin dreams as they withdrew like the waves, seeing if any of them were carrying any useful flotsam that might be saved and yarned about. None did. But with the rising of the light through the bedroom windows I mused upon Raasay again, rather regretting that I'd read all the now-defunct on-line journals and would no longer be peering at them.

It's been a pleasant experience for me, gazing into that island at various levels. I'm reminded of the belief that in the realm between lives you can look 'down' into your next one and choose accordingly. Looking into Raasay has been like this and, in a moment of sleepy whimsy, I wondered if that is where I will find myself reborn. I think I'd like that.

Mind you in Lyn Buchanan's *Seventh Sense* that I quoted earlier, he described tracking souls from their moment of death and actually reincarnating in times that were *earlier* than their present lives. I don't want to be born there during The Clearances. I wouldn't mind being born when Moluag went there and I'd help him with his chapel and boat, and listen to what he had to offer. Not sure if I'll get a choice though, depending on what I make of my own karma.

But what about Morgana le Fay?!

All of us can swept along by the sheer, sexy power of her Myth but during the writing of this book, she hasn't really touched me at all. I no longer feel the urge to get to Brittany. Perhaps I met an echo of her within Christine Hartley, as her Magical Diaries show, and that's probably all I need. I suppose it might seem a cop-out by saying that I should now try to find Morgana le Fay within myself rather than 'out there', but I can't offer more than that yet. Maybe next year when we do get into the tantalisingly dark heart of Northgalis (North Wales) I might see Morgana's green eyes and her long, beckoning finger, but until then I'll just carry on being fascinated by the more solid Mysteries of Nature and the sheer impermeable Magick of the Land.

As for Moluag, dear Lua, I've thoroughly enjoyed sharing his boat. Has he been a real, psychic, inner plane 'contact' of the sort that Seymour and Hartley would commune with? Of the sort that *you* can meet? I really don't know. I can only say that by acting 'as if' he were, then all sorts of things have presented themselves to me.

I can only now channel Lua in a whimsical sense and say to any reader who is still with me:

Dia is Muire duit...God and Mary be with you...

THE ELEMENTAL RAY
by F.P.D.
(Col. C.R.F. Seymour)

aka Kim's Book

In this manual of self-initiation, Seymour maintained that a group of two or three people working together, or even an individual reading the material and brooding over it on his own, could produce a great release of energy that is tied up within the soul of the average Westerner. This in turn would make a considerable difference to the amount of positive force available to him for creativity in his life. As he writes within this long essay: 'Now this study in moon symbols is intended to show the reader a way of initiation. If studied with care it will enable a self-initiation into the symbolism of the moon cult to take place.'

I don't think there is anyone, after reading this, who has not tried to get to the Cave in the Mountain, find the Watcher at the Ford of the Moon and go beyond there to the High Place of the Moon within the realms of the Fae.

Bear in mind that this was written in the late 1930s, and you should make appropriate allowances for Seymour's Irish-Anglo mindset and Jungian terminology.

INTRODUCTION

What follows is a study in imagery. It has been written around the results of experiments in group meditation using ancient pagan symbols. These experiments had for their objective the linking up of memories dormant in the unconscious minds of the members that still live in the unconscious mind of the Great Mother of all-that-exists on this planet.

Most of the members of these groups have, in the past, served at the altars of pagan religions and have met, face to face, the shining ones of the forests and the mountains, of the lakes and the seas. Such memories never die either *Here* or *Yonder,* and they live because of their power, or shall it be said, their vital energy. They are *Within* man's memory, as well as *Without* him in the memory of our Great Mother, who is called the Lady of Nature, the Bona Dea, the Magna Mater, Isis.

In the course of these experiments it was discovered that if any one of the members of a group had in the past a strong contact with a particular cult at a certain period, that individual could communicate these memories to others, and could link them with the cult memories that still lie within the Earth memories of Isis as the Lady of Nature.

At first difficulties, contradictions and disappointments were many. It was almost impossible to distinguish between fancy and the results obtained by the imagination trained magically. Then, as the result of years of work carefully recorded, a system of cross-checking grew up, and in the experimental work of these groups a reasonable degree of probability was obtained. One discovery was made that cleared up many contradictions. Religions change their status. Bergson's philosophical concept of life as an ever-becoming applies to religions, to the Gods, both great and small, as well as to an individual man. Also every man's concept of a God is an ever-becoming, even when that man proclaims that his God is Being or the very Essence of Being. Man creates his own Gods.

From this conception of religions as changing without cessation gradually grew, for us, the idea of the Religions of the High-roads and the Religions of the By-roads, an interesting theme that will be developed in more detail. It will be sufficient to point out here that most great religions start in their youth as religions of the by-road. In maturity they become one of the great religions of the High Road , and in old age they return to the obscurity of the by-road. Yet strange as this statement may sound, it is in the cults of the by-ways that power (not material power however) is greatest.

The members taking part in these experiments have in the past served at the altars of these cults of the by-ways. And again and again, life after life there comes the necessity for making the choice between the popular religion of the high-road, and the religion of the by-road which is despised and rejected by worldly men.

A study of the history of religion shows that the way of heresy usually is the way of the by-road, and, since the Prince of Peace came, the by-road has only too often been the high-road to the stake or gallows. Before the Prince of Peace came history tells us that cults and religions often changed their status. For example at one time the cults of Isis and Osiris were religions of the high-road. Times changed and the cult of Isis became the cult of the simpler folk living in the villages and the country. To use a modern term the religion of Isis became pagan, that is the religion of the paganus or the country folk. Still later Isis-worship once again became fashionable and She developed into the divine ruler of most Mediterranean civilisation. Isis today lives on in the modern cult of the Virgin Mother of God, rightly beloved by certain sections of Christianity.

The feminine cults or Woman's Mysteries when working with the ancient moon symbolism are, even today in so-called Christian England, exceedingly potent as a means for obtaining and using the 'energies' of the Inner Worlds on what the Qabalists call the level of Yesod. But this aspect of life is, and usually remains, a *terra incognita* so far as the rich, the prosperous, and the happy are concerned. Isis was, and still is, the Divine Consolatrix. The powers of Isis are often to be found manifesting through the old hag in the hut - they are not very often given to the fashionable woman in her town house.

It is more easy to get in touch with the Isis power by tapping the memories that pertain to a period when the Isis cult belonged to the religions of the by-way, when it was neglected by the wealthy, the educated and the hierarchical classes who lived in or near the great Egyptian towns. This too is a theme that will be developed later when dealing with the old conflict between Patriarchy and Matriarchy. For it is *the* woman that holds the keys of the inner planes for *a* man. If you want to pass the Cumaean Gates you must become as a little child and a woman must lead you. You must find your Deiphobe, you must turn up the by-way that leads over the wild heather-clad heaths, you must pass through the forests, you must sacrifice to the Goddess of Three Ways, if you would reach the 'Cave in the Mountains'.

'Cherchez la femme!' has a hidden meaning which is known only to the initiate who understands the significance of Omar Khayam's lament:

> *There was a door to which I had no key,*
> *There was a veil past which I could not see.*

It was Deiphobe, daughter of Glaucus, priestess of Phoebus, and of the Goddess of Three Ways who, for King Aeneas, opened the keyless door and drew the veil that hides life from death, and death from Life.

THE CAVE IN THE MOUNTAIN

> Another way went Aeneas the true, to the towering fastness where Apollo reigns, and, near, that monstrous cavern, dread Sibyl's seclusion; where he of Delos, he the prophet, breathes into her spirit's visionary might, revealing things to come. Now they came near the woods of the goddess of Three Ways and near that house of gold.
>   'Cumaean Gates,'by W.F.J. Knight, pages XIV and XV.

In lives that now belong to the distant past most of those who today seek to leave the broad highways of the orthodox World Religions and to adventure along the various by-paths that lead to the Cave in the Mountain have served at altars belonging to Woman's Mysteries. The key to these mysteries is only to be found in the dark cave that lies in a wooded ravine just beneath a tree-crowned summit.

Nevertheless it is freely admitted that the great religions of the high-roads have their part to play in civilization, and a very important one it is. For not only do they shepherd their sheep along a broad and safe track, but they also are naturally conservative and so are a guard against spiritual anarchy. Organized religions make excellent ballast.

From the psychological point of view as taught in the Mystery Schools the conscious mind of man is considered to be predominantly male while the subconscious mind is usually considered to be largely female. The subconscious mind is, as is well known, a storehouse of emotional power. It is the source of that energy which drives a man into action. It might almost be called the human power-house. In the same way the generating station for the power that animates the group soul of any nation lies in its subconscious. If the argument that has been put forward is historically and actually sound then the driving-power of the English people lies in the Celtic potentialities of its group soul.

Today, if woman is to regain in religion the honoured place she once so worthily held, she must turn up the by-way that leads through the woods, over the wild heaths, to the Cave in the Mountain. There and there only will she gain the freedom that once was hers. There, through learning the wisdom that is taught in the Cave in the Mountain will she regain her ancient power, her religious freedom, and the spiritual prestige which is hers because she is spiritually the stronger and intuitively the wiser sex.

Man creates theologies; Woman is Religion. In the realms of religion man, if left to himself, is only too often content to remain in a bog that is named Psychical Research. Deiphobe, daughter of Glaucus, put the matter very neatly to King Aeneas when she said impatiently: 'Non hoc ista sibi tempus spectacula poscit.' (Now is no time that commands staring at sights, as you stare.)

If a man wishes to pass the Cumaean Gates he must first leave the highways of religion and seek the by-ways that run steeply upwards through the woods of the Goddess of Three Ways. But let him not forget as he enters Her woods that a woman must lead him if he wishes to pass through the Cumaean Gates; for Cumae is, for us, a western land of death and re-birth. The Druids taught this in the story of Connla and the Lady of the Sidhe. Jung explains it in his preface to the *Secret of the Golden Flower*. Practical experience in group meditation confirms its truth.

It takes two, a positive and a negative, to make an efficiently functioning psychic unit.

As Dr. Harding has so clearly pointed out in *Woman's Mysteries* the worship of the Moon Goddess was an education of the emotional life by means of a series of initiations. An initiation ceremony may be acted upon the physical stage in a dramatized myth, but initiation *per se* is an education of the emotions and its field of experience is in the unconscious mind. Its culmination (which the ancients called the summons of the God or Goddess) takes place, sometimes before, sometimes not until long after the physical plane ceremonies have ended. For these latter are only intended to stir the *heart* of the man, that is, his subconscious mind. Initiation is not a ceremony, it is the beginning of a new way of using the mind.

Now this study in moon symbols is intended to show the reader a way of initiation. If studied with care it will enable a self-initiation into the symbolism of the moon cult to take place. For by means of a system for the training of the image-making faculty, unconscious memories that have been gradually accumulated over a long series of lives are stirred up and brought into consciousness.

As a study in imagery, in order to practice 'composition of place' as described by Ignatius Loyola, build in detail the following word pictures as if you were preparing them in your mind before setting them out on the stage of a theatre. Picture clearly each of the characters in the various scenes and then try to live yourself into these scenes AS IF you were one of the principal characters, and taking in the first place the character that most of all appeals to you.

This study is meant as an exercise in practical meditation upon the information that has so far been given you. Invent as pleases you little turns and twists to make the scenes and the characters live more clearly. But at the same time it must be remembered that, as mental and emotional training, this type of meditation is potent for good or ill. It embodies much of the practical technique that is used in Mystery Schools, and if persevered in, it will bring the student out of the highway and on to the by-way that rightly is his.

Let it never be forgotten that a man is what subconsciously he pictures himself to be. For as Coué discovered, the unconscious wish is more potent than the conscious intention.

EXERCISE 1

THE BY-ROAD TO THE CAVE IN THE MOUNTAIN

Along the border of a wide, green and fertile plain rises a range of high hills with many steep jungle-covered spurs that are separated by deep ravines which run far up into a mountainous country that lies to the North. Picture range after range rising between you and the perpetual snows that glisten and sparkle upon the far distant northern horizon. Vivid green are the lower slopes that come down into this rich and well-watered plain. Brown and russet are the bare crags. Blue is the sky that overhangs the peaks, their ridges, and the rivers to which they give rise. Bright are the colours of this hidden land that abuts on silver and purple Yesod.

Across this plain and up the widest of these blue-misted valleys runs a broad road built carefully to a very gentle slope. The eye cannot see whence it comes, whither it goes is also unknown. Its beginning and ending are incomprehensible for they are lost in that illusion which the conscious mind calls time and space. And the reason why you and the rest of humanity have to travel this road is beyond human understanding while still in the flesh. All that any one can surmise is that having climbed those far-of snow-clad heights, man sheds his humanity and prepares to take upon himself Divinity. Even now potentially man is as the Elohim, and we know not what we shall be then.

Having carefully constructed in the mind's eye this brightly coloured picture, continue for several days to build and rebuild it until as soon as you turn your attention upon it as a completed picture it will spring into being within you. Next proceed to elaborate this picture; then analyse your reactions to it and to the pictures that rise from your unconscious mind as you think upon it and noting most particularly the colours in which the latter show themselves. These latter as your own personal contribution to the process are very important for your mental tone will colour them brightly or otherwise.

The road itself is crowded with a long serpent-like column that slowly moves northward towards those distant snows. This column is composed of men, women and children. It is humanity seeking experience in the process of evolution, usually, as the Buddha taught, through self-inflicted suffering.

The Great Mother has children other than humans. And winding up other valleys that lie to the right and the left of that up which climbs humanity are yet other roads. These too are broad and gentle of slope. Up them, in a manner similar to humanity, toil 'your brethren of the other evolutions'. They are hidden from sight by steep jungle-clad ridges and humanity as a whole knows nothing of them.

There are however individuals who have left the main column on the high road and have climbed up the mountain side to the white temple of Diana of the Three Ways. These individuals on that sacred tree-clad mountain top have, in the House of Gold, received from the priestess of Phoebus the gift of clear vision. It is however a vision which is not just mere seeing; for it is a gift which enables the one who has received it worthily to become aware of many non-human aspects of the One Divine Life of the Many Breasted One. For She too is seeking experience by means of an ever-becoming. Nothing in that Divine Life which ever flows from the sacred black and white breasts is stable. Everything that has life and can reflect upon itself can ascertain this one thing for itself - 'Je change sans cesse'. Her life is change, and with cessation of change Her life comes out of the YONDER, disappears, and its form fades out from our view HERE.

Now picture yourself as moving upon that road, a unit of that column. Imagine clearly what you can see and feel. Next try to catch hold of the thoughts that would fill your mind as suddenly and upon an impulse you step out of the caravan on to the grassy edge and watch it roll slowly past you. You are now a spectator but they are busy living each their own life in that column. It may come as a shock to you to notice that you are now outside the herd. You are alone, and it is said that the lone wolf away from the pack, as a rule, perishes quickly.

Is that to be your fate? That sudden impulse which made you, at a certain spot, step out from the main column is the stirring of old memories. And it is well to pause and realize this stage with the utmost thoroughness for it is here that the soul takes up once again THE PATH. It is here that it is necessary to learn to be alone yet not lonely. It is here that one surmises that for each one of us life holds a special type of experience, something has to be done but no one else can do it for one. It is here that people begin to look askance at the one who watches the herd from outside the line of its march. Then there are the guardians of the caravan, to whom the caravan pays reverence, calling them its priests. These guardians look at you uneasily. The unwise guardian seeks to head you back into the column, the wise guardian watches to see that you do not seduce others who are in his charge.

See yourself watching and waiting expectantly. Then a little later feel yourself wanting to rejoin the column and wondering what all the bother is about - for nothing happens - just yet.

Loneliness and boredom are always the primary experiences of the path, and it is well to be prepared for them. As you gaze about you wondering why you obeyed that sudden impulse, you see a narrow path leading up the hillside. There is a notice at its entrance - 'No Road. Trespassers will be Persecuted'. This path is forbidden, and immediately a dark-clad guardian warns you that travel by this road means madness, disgrace, perdition, hell for ever and ever.

Now if you believe him you had better hurry back to the main body. You may not attempt that by-road in safety until you realize clearly and fully that each man is his own saviour. You are your own priest; no one, except yourself, can stand between you and your own divinity. Potentially you are divine, but actually you are as yet only human. This is the age of Aquarius; the age of the free man who carrying his own burdens on his own shoulders strides manfully across the sky. The age of Aquarius is to be the age that will free man from the bogies of any outworn superstitions.

If free from these superstitions, then press boldly up the path until a plateau forming a halting place that overlooks the main road is reached. This plateau, the first stage leading to The Path, is occupied by an arguing crowd that disputes vigorously, and its members are as dogmatic and fanatical over their particular doctrines as the guardians of the high- way. For they have not yet discovered that the quarrelsome are not really on the Path that leads to an inner freedom.

There is a steep track leading up the hill from this plateau and it is closed by a gate. its Guardian asks you what you know. He does not want your beliefs. He wants to know your knowledge, if you have any – and until you can distinguish between belief and knowledge you may not pass him.

You will also be asked your motive for seeking this particular by-path. And the only answer that will open the gate is:

'I desire to know in order to serve.'

Any other motive is considered to be impure for only the pure in subconscious intention (this the ancients called the heart) can, with safety, invoke the powers of the Bona Dea who was and still is the Celtic Goddess Anu or Annis, Dana: Isis of many names.

Having passed the first gate a long and steep climb leads to another plateau, which appears to be empty, except for a small bench which is just long enough to seat two. Sitting on this bench one can see the column far below; its advance guard is beyond view and its rear guard is not within view.

'All will reach their destination - in time,' says a voice. And then a stranger draws attention to a notice-board marked with an arrow that points straight up the mountain and bearing the inscription: 'To the Cave on the Mountain'.

If questioned the stranger will say that in this cave is to be found Wisdom: the Wisdom of the Cave in the Mountain. He will also explain that this path is called the path of death in life. In any case he will point out that this hill cannot be climbed alone; the Wisdom of the Cave in the Mountain is not for any man who is a solitary: 'for that which is solitary is barren'.

This stranger will tell you to return to the high-road and to get a woman, who if she is the woman of your choice and you are the man of her choice may be an unknowing Eve or a very knowing Lilith. It matters not in actual practice which she is, for women are intuitive and adaptable, and usually take to the routine of the PATH more quickly, though perhaps less thoroughly, than a man.

But back to the high-road you must go until you have found what is, in truth, your better half for Anima and Animus must be MATED, so that the ONE becomes the TWO and the TWO are FOUR.

THE WATCHER AT THE FORD OF THE MOON

At the end of each day when he goes to bed a would-be Magus, as a symbolic action should wipe his brow with the back of his hand and say to himself: 'Has my brow this day been wet with mental sweat?' This little rite has value not only as a reminder of the Great Work that has been undertaken, but also as a mental and emotional catharsis, for it has been

115

truly said that the chief temptation of any would-be Magus is creation without mental toil.

Now these exercises although they are elementary involve an intensive and somewhat unusual mental effort. Their object is, by the use of symbols and imagery, to enable the reader to deduce from the content of his own unconscious mind much that has hitherto lain fallow. A technique is set forth first by giving the principles upon which it is based, and then by showing in an actual meditation how such a technique is to be used. The result should be that by visualizing each exercise carefully and accurately, a freeing of the unconscious mind takes place. The dark prison in which the frustrated emotions are shut up is opened, the life-force flows OUT with greater freedom, and mental energy is thus released.

This technique has been used for some years. The records of its successes and its failures cover thousands of pages, and they represent many hours of both group and solitary meditation, for the students who have taken part in them can be counted by the score. It is advisable, at first, to stick closely to the methods as given here, but later on when more proficient, each student should work out for himself the technique that suits him best, for Moon Mysteries have widely varying stories to tell to the many different kinds of souls that seek their initiation in Yesod, the sphere of the Moon, where the Moon Goddesses are each of triple figure - dark and destructive in waning, bright and constructive in waxing, integrating and perfective at the full. And this is true psychologically as well as cosmically.

Meditation in Moon Mysteries may be defined briefly as the pursuit of inner active objectives. And in some of the quieter moments of deep meditation, which is an inner process that is not externalized, one becomes at times very strongly aware of an observer. He (or it!) almost seems to be something or someone that is external to oneself. Some authorities consider this to be an entity external to that Unity which is a MAN. Others consider the observer be the Higher Self that forever dwells in the most secret recesses of a man's being. Really it is the conscious finding of this hidden one that is important, the labelling is actually of little value, and it does not matter if he be YOU or NOT-YOU.

We think of Man as a unity which consists of a Cosmic Atom that is unmanifest and has its home in spheres that are utterly beyond all human conception. This Cosmic Atom or Monad, as some name it, has no beginning and no ending as limited human reason conceives of these two things. It sends forth from its own essential being what is called a Higher Self or Genius, an individuality, which is an ever-changing entity that evolves through the immensely long period that a man has to spend in the

116

bosom of the Great Mother in order to gain his full quota of experience as a unit of the human race.

This Individuality or Genius in its turn sends forth from itself a portion of its own substance which is called the Lower Self, and this latter is that natural phenomenon which is known during earth life as Mr. Jones or Miss Smith. And let it be said (you can disagree if you like for no proof is possible) that as Mr. Jones and Miss Smith you incarnate. But Miss Smith and Mr. Jones only incarnate. THEY NEVER REINCARNATE. It is the Higher Self of each one of us that seeks re-incarnation by incarnating a little bit at a time. And the non-incarnating portion of Miss Smith and Mr. Jones is the Observer, the Guardian at the Gate, etc.

The older, wiser and more perfectly human a soul seems to be, the greater is the extent to which the Higher Self is able to shine through its temporarily incarnated Personality. Man is an integral unity, though there are some that would deny this statement, but for the purpose of empirical instruction it is customary to think of him in this threefold fashion.

First, the Personality is the unit of evolution for the period of a single incarnation on the material planet Earth. It is the Miss Smith or Mr. Jones of everyday waking conscious life. Second, the Individuality is the unit of evolution for that immensely long period which the Hindus and Theosophists call a Manvantara, or in terms of the Western tradition, a 'Day of the Gods'. It (the Individuality) is our Virgin Mother, the immeasurably ancient, very wise, infinitely patient Watcher at the Gates of the Unseen; the Judge who has to be faced at Death. Third, the Cosmic Atom or Monad is the unit of a period of evolution so immense and of such divine, supra-human potentialities that we call it Unmanifest, and label it indescribable.

The above is a simple and convenient empirical system for beginners. There is no need for the student to believe in it. It may be, perhaps, 1% accurate, and it is almost certainly 99% inadequate, but if used intelligently as a convenient working hypothesis, it will enable the student to co-operate with his own far wiser 'Watcher at the Threshold'. To learn how to use this system is the first step that has to be taken when on the path of the Moon Mysteries that leads to An-na-Rea - The Ford of the Lord of the Moon according to the Celtic Mystery teaching.

After meditation - but not during it – when analysing and comparing, and during the process of recording results, watch carefully for 'The Observer' and the part that he has played. Also watch the inside of your own soul and see WHO has been there.

Now having studied these brief and elementary points with regard to the art of meditation, it is necessary for the student to think very carefully about the relationship between the Watcher and that which is called the Universal Subconsciousness.

Behind the physical body that each of us inhabits during this our earthly life is a purposive Entity that may in some far distant aeon transcend the limitations of human intelligence and begin a new stage of evolution as a Divine intelligence.

In the subconscious depths of the human mind lie hidden all the experiences of humanity, for there is the subconsciousness of humanity as well as the subconscious of a human being. Man is an integral part of that greater whole which is called the human race, and the theory that there is racial subconscious common to all humanity is fairly generally accepted because it explains much that is not easy otherwise to understand.

Behind this physical earth that we and other evolutions inhabit during physical existence, is a purposive Entity that is divine: a non-human Entity that is intelligent and evolves through the expression of its own essential nature. As man evolves through an ever-becoming, so also this Entity, which we call the Great Mother, Great Isis, Dana, and by many other names, evolves by means of an 'ever-becoming'. The Law of Ceaseless Change is the law of Her being just as it is the law of that much smaller Entity – Man.

This does not mean that the Divine functions according to limitations that are set by human reason. The functions are analogous, which is not the same as identical.

'As above, so below,' is a very ancient maxim which in effect means that man is a microcosm of the universe or macrocosm. Man's mind is an integral portion of that larger whole which is called the Universal Mind: man's subconsciousness is an integral portion of a much greater collective subconscious; man's memory is an integral part of a much wider universal memory in exactly the same way that man's life in an integral and indivisible part of the Universal Life, and man's material body is an integral and indivisible part of the material body of the Earth Entity.

This as a method of description is, of course, pure anthropomorphism, and quite rightly should be condemned as such for anthropomorphism in an unreflecting way of thinking is deplorable. But in meditation, especially in its deeper levels, anthropomorphism works most successfully. And until you have found empirically some other and better method of working, you will have to be content with this anthropomorphic method if you wish to have life and power in your work. If meditation subjects are purely abstract ideas or just ethical, this question will not arise, because imagination is not being exercised.

Nevertheless, practical experience, which has been carefully recorded immediately, will soon teach that any real depth of communion with the Great Mother, with Isis as Nature, is only possible on the condition that one works with Her as if she were like unto Man, though of course without mankind's all too obvious, mental, emotional, and spiritual limitations.

Many years of experience has taught that if you want to meditate in a manner that will spiritualise and intensify as well as recreate your mental life you will have, in actual practical work, to make use of the two following maxims as if they were true:

(i) There is a Principle of Life which is universal; it fills all space and it is immanent in all forms. The substance of this Principle of Life is Mind.
(ii) Man's mind is an integral portion of this Universal Mind.

If these two maxims are true, and practical experience seems to show that they work as if they were natural laws, then all idea of mental separateness is an illusion. All minds are joined together as integral parts of a complete whole. They are parts of the Universal Mind as waves are parts of the sea.

When a man is meditating with power, his mind is in action and affects its surroundings in this sea of universal mind-stuff in much the same way that the propellers of a ship churn the ocean through which it is passing. Steam sets the 'propellers working. Imagination fired by desire drives the human mind into purposive mental action. Imagination driven by desire is almost always stronger than mere reason; as Ignatius taught: 'ACT AS IF . . .

It is well to remember that just as a man's mind is an integral part of the mind of Nature, i.e. of Isis as Mother Earth, so, in turn, Her mind is part of a still greater Mind that is in its own degree universal, and so on ad infinitum.

Be spacious in your outlook on infinity, remembering that the cosmic outlook of an earth-worm is probably but little less narrow than is a man's outlook when compared with the cosmic consciousness of such a Divine Being as the Great Mother. After all, it is true that all knowledge is purely relative.

When contemplating the gifts of the Great Mother that are to be obtained through meditation it must be kept in mind once and for ever that one's meditation is not done for one's own personal benefit. This life force must not be drawn upon selfishly, but only to enable the life of the Great Mother to flow more freely, to manifest more strongly. The object should be for each in his own small way TO ENABLE THE GREAT GODDESS TO LIVE MORE PERFECTLY THE EXPERIENCE SHE NEEDS FOR HER OWN DEVELOPMENT.

There is no need to accept these hypotheses as true, but better results are to be got in one's practical work if they be accepted and used as if they were true.

EXERCISE II.

AT THE FORD OF THE MOON

The man found his woman. As a modern Adam and Eve going back to THE GARDEN of the Great Mother they left the second plateau above the High-way by a path that ran through a steep cleft in the hills and up on to a spur covered with rocks and dark juniper and small green thorn trees. There, taking breath, they looked about them.

In front, but some little distance away, is open country, a wild broken heath-land basking in a sunset glow of green and gold. Its shallow valleys are filled with a light mist of turquoise blue. Its heather-covered spurs slope gradually upward to the crescent-shaped ridge of Drum-na-Rea, the Ridge of the Moon.

Behind them no portion of the broad High-road is to be seen, no sound of the tramping of weary feet upon its hard surface breaks the fairy-like silence of this green, grassy by-way. The alchemical operation of SOLVE has been carried out. A new land has been entered. The frontiers of the country of the High-way have gently closed behind them, and strange by-roads lead down into the greater freedom of 'the Oldest Land'.

Below them is a shallow valley filled with green beech and oak woods that are slightly veiled in a faintly violet mist. The path turns down suddenly and steeply into this valley which it apparently crosses, for the narrow ribbon of the green by-way can be seen winding up the heath towards the centre of the ridge of Drum-na-Rea.

After a pause the man and the woman he has chosen to   *be his guide leave the spur and turn down the path that enters the wood. Once within that warm, moist atmosphere it feels as if one had gone into another dimension of soft, green, translucent spaces, spaces that are very still and windless, yet they seem to reflect something that is vividly alive. One gets the impression of looking into the green and pale blue depths of a woodland pond that is reflecting the sky and the aliveness of the green leaves above its surface. This is the Fairy Greenwood that surrounds An-*

na-Rea, the Ford of the Moon. It is lit by an inner light of brilliant fairy gold and

green, in which phantom-like forms appear only to disappear once attention is consciously directed upon them.

Actually nothing is heard, nothing is seen, but it feels as if many unseen Presences, hoping for recognition, are waiting just behind this veil of green stillness to greet these wanderers from the broad high-way of everyday experience.

In spite of the utter absence of any visible form of movement, the wood appears to be pulsating with life. The trees are motionless in the early evening stillness, yet the tree folk children of Dana, the Great Mother, are holding their evening revel. One is never quite sure, until it vanishes when one stares hard, whether a tree is really a

so-called inanimate thing of wood and soft green leaves, or a vast, tenuous, brightly coloured living Elemental with an almost human-like form that seems to slip in and out of the imprisoning bark.

Laughing Dryads, if not watched too intently, seem to peep and peer with the curiosity and shyness of wild things from behind the thick bales of beech and oak; the ferns and bracken are alive with the smaller fairy folk all waiting for their play-time. Fauns with tiny knob-like horns people these green spaces that seem to close in upon one as if a wall of transparent, tenuous, very still water was preparing slowly and gently to pour through this wood which is now a fairy wood that is coloured with the greenish starlight of Netzach, the sphere of the Elemental Gods who are the Shining Ones that wear emerald green robes. The note of this wood is that of friendliness, for all its dimly seen inhabitants are glad that this man and woman have come away from the hard glare of the great white high-way into the softly shining greenness of the Celtic Twilight. All around are the 'Children of Other Evolutions' ready to greet these accredited newcomers as their Brethren. For, have not they also for their Divine Parent, the Great Mother, the Green Isis, ruler of the still,transparent, shadowy green woods and all that therein dwell!

> *Give to these children, new from the world,*
> *Silence and love;*
> *And the long dew-dropping hours of the night,*
> *And the stars above...*

sings W.B. Yeats in 'A Faery Song' sung by people of faery over Diarmid and Grania in their bridal sleep under a cromlech.

On the short sward some little distance away stands Caoilte [pronounced Kiltë], a royal figure with hair burning as if touched by a last golden ray of sunlight. He is clad in green and gold with a spear in his hand and a rounded shield slung on his left arm. As Lord of the fairy wood he gives greeting, and then turns to the West. He passes down the wood, saluted by all, for is he not the Prince of the Sidhe! [Shee] He halts in a wide, open glade through which a deep stream glides silently and without ripple. In the brown of this clear bog-water is reflected the still sun-lit evening sky as well as a great golden harvest moon. For this is the season when the moonlight and the twilight of early Autumn strive for mastery, the fairy time when 'The Host is rushing 'twixt night and day'.

This glade is called An-na-Rea, the Ford of the Moon. Caoilte points with his spear into the dark, shining depths and bids the pair of humans look therein. The man, his thoughts bent on climbing the distant hill whereon is the temple of the Goddess of Three Ways, sees but a long dark ridge mirrored in the still water, and the shimmering silver-shining rays of the round golden-silvery moon that is Her symbol. But the woman, more open to the fiery fairy magnetism that flows from the golden leader of the Host that is in Knock-na-Rea, has seen in its deeps the glitter of the green and golden palaces of the Sidhe.

In a flash, without breaking the still surface by even a single ripple, she has dived deep into the fairy pool and down, far down, into that fifth dimensional world which the Irish Celts call Tir-na-mbeo (the Land of the Ever-Youthful).

'Your guide has proved more clear of sight than you,' explains Caoilte. 'Yet look not behind you, but cross by the moon-bridge if you can.'

A white moon-mist gathers upon the water; it swirls up into an arch and forms the moon-bridge over An-na-Rea. Alone the crossing is made and the western bank is reached.

Caoilte too has gone, but in his place is a woman of the Sidhe holding a branch of silver-like blossom.

THE WATCHER, HIS SYMBOLS AND SYMBOL SYSTEM

The process through which is developed an awareness of the 'Watcher Within' is meditation.

The tools that are used in this process are symbols and symbol systems. These are usually borrowed from active existing systems or from the so-called dead religious systems of the childhood of man. These ancient systems however are not dead. They are merely quiescent in so far as the ordinary man is concerned. For those who make a comparative study of the psychology of myth they are dormant like the sleeping princess in a fairy tale; but they can be awakened into an intense spiritual, mental and emotional activity when the right stimulus is given at the right time.

Jung in the chapters on the 'Symbolism of the Mother and of Rebirth' and 'The Song of the Moth' in his valuable and suggestive book 'The Psychology of the Unconscious' has set forth an almost inexhaustible supply of ideas that will repay careful and open-minded reflection in the quiet moments of meditation.

Now 'conditioning' is the first and the most important process in the art of using symbols. Unless you are conditioned to a symbol and can react to it either in an orthodox or unorthodox manner (it matters not which) it is not for you a symbol. A symbol must bring to mind active qualities. It is not just a portrait.

A symbol may have many meanings and these may vary in different persons. Take the symbol ♀ which is but a circle above a cross. For the zoologist this means a female as opposed to ♂ a male. For the poet ♀ means a pleasant form of restlessness that usually attacks a young man in the early Spring of each year. Astronomers and astrologers use it for the planet Venus, but each gives to it a different content. The astronomer thinks of ♀ as a bright body in the sky. For the astrologer ♀ denotes certain tidal energies in an ever-flowing cosmic life stream that comes from the Unmanifest source of all life.

It may be just as well to point out here, for it is an important point that is often forgotten that the educated astrologers know well that the planet ♀ no more causes these cosmic tides than the Roman numeral I on the face of the clock in the dining~room, causes lunch! The immediate cause of lunch is the cook, who remains, so far as the dining-room clock is concerned, in a state of unmanifestatlon in another dimension - the kitchen!

If this idea be extended to other symbols and groups of symbols it soon becomes evident that the importance of a symbol lies in what you learn about it. You can learn much from reading books, but you can learn a great deal more by turning over in quiet and regular meditation the knowledge you have already acquired from sources external to yourself.

Now meditation in its early stages is a training in the art of using symbols. And the details of the examples and exercises which are given at the end of each section should be repeatedly studied with care for many days in succession for they are exercises that have been used with good results in both solitary and group meditation. Never forget that if you want to become familiar with a symbol you must meditate upon it again and again and again. Follow the example of Napoleon who said: 'Read and re-read.' His method of reading was really, as he himself has told us, a system for training his visualising imagination, and his re-reading took the form of a visualising meditation. A symbol is meant to be incubated over a considerable period if it is to be hatched out into action.

In pursuit of these inner active objectives it can be said truly that in most cases (i.e. for the ordinary individual) it is better to work strictly to a daily time-table, as well as to sit in a comfortable chair where the body is forgotten. Ten minutes daily methodical work done thus in consciously directed exercise is usually worth ten times as many hours done without method when the whim to meditate is felt.

These visualising exercises seek to present the internal activities of the meditative life, and their repercussions upon the physical make-up of the student, with a reasonable clarity and in such a way that he can understand with ease what is being done. Making a clear presentation to another or even to oneself is not an easy thing to do, for the realities of the internal activities of meditation are not to be described by means of a language that is limited to objects in three dimensions. Such realities can only be described by means of analogy. For example the moon is often used for the group soul of women as a class: then the moon is dynamic. Materially speaking, the moon in the sky is a passive ball of rock which as a cold dead sphere reflects the light of the sun. In the former case, though a three-dimensional language is used, one is not dealing with science nor with facts, but with delicate and all but intangible feelings and moods and yearnings that are peculiar to a group soul and to the individuals who make up that group entity.

One talks of woods and marshes, of fords and ridges, and of horned moons, but it is the effect (upon the subconscious mind of the reader) that is produced by the inner substance or the essence of these material things as holy places that is being referred to here, and not just their three-dimensional externals that are so fully and carefully outlined. The outer symbol is described with what may seem to many as unnecessary wealth of detail, which is often repeated with intention, because it is by these means that subconscious feeling and emotion are stirred up. This deliberate repetition is an important part of the process and it should be studied carefully, for the subconscious always works in terms of picture consciousness and it is the representations of colours and sounds and smells that tug most effectively at the strings of its memory.

The symbol of the physical moon and certain colour effects are described again and again. Not however in careless repetition, but deliberately, in order to stir up the energies of the sphere of Yesod that dwells in the soul of man as a microcosm of the macrocosm. The object is to call into activity the immensely dynamic and purposive inner nature of BOTH these spheres of sensation, for one is subjective and the other objective in a meditation. Here is the same idea as that of shattering a glass by the repeated sounding of its note. For the sphere of the moon within the sphere of sensation (subjective) of the soul of a man is directly linked to the moon sphere that is within the soul (objective) of the Planetary Spirit of this earth, and the physical moon is thus but the symbol of that cosmic tide which then acts upon man's subconscious moonsphere. The rise of the tide in the North Sea will fill a London Dock that is many miles away from the coast but still in connection with the sea. And so it happens when the soul of a man is linked consciously with the soul of our Great Mother – Nature - Her tidalflow becomes our tidalflow - Her life is consciously felt in our life.

Once you have thoroughly mastered this system you can begin to build these images in your own way, and thus put the stamp of your own individuality into all your work. For if this is not done you can never become a true Magus and nothing that is real can be achieved by you, for you are working mechanically and without inspiration. Inspiration is the result of repeated efforts, and with it you create magically a something that will work quite independent of your volition. This something is what the priests of the Old Religion sought deliberately to create for use in their rites, rituals, and meditations. It is the link between the Magus and the cosmic energy he seeks to use. In the Old Religion the object of the priest or priestess was to work with inspiration, that is, with the inbreathing of a cosmic energy which was deliberately visualized and intentionally invoked.

Let the motto of a would-be-Magus be: *Labor omnia vincit.* Act and react to these inner representations until you have lost all sense of the HOW, the WHEN and the WHERE in the feelings spontaneously created within you by these visions which have been so often built up mechanically by daily mental toil. When this happens a re-presentation is no longer just your subjective mental picture. It has become (for you) an entity which is not only objective but also vibrant with life, and it is real upon its own plane of being, though that is not this material plane of physical sensation.

When this happens you have taken the first long step that leads to self-mastery as a true Magus: that is, as a person who has trained his unconscious mind to create by means of the ancient technique of the Westem Mystery Tradition; a technique that is, in its own way, as sound for us as is that of Eastern Yoga for the peoples of Asia.

With the flowering of the powers of the subconscious mind comes inspiration, and then the Magus pours into the visions that he is creating ALL the energies of his own soul. Read Ezekiel's vision of the Valley of Dry Bones. [Ezekiel, Chap. 37.] Then very carefully visualize it, for you have in it, barely hidden behind a transparent veil of commonplace words, a practical magical technique with each step described in detail and the final result clearly indicated. There is much magical lore in the seemingly strange tales of the Hebrew Bible.

Working in this way, the would-be-Magus is developing in a perfectly safe manner his own inner life. With steady development character is being rounded off and matured. This development will tend to show itself in his mundane activities.

Thus one gives life to one's visions by living them in meditation and in ritual with a desire that is made as strong as possible, even if in the early stages such desire may have to be stimulated artificially. The vision is lived by experiencing its appropriate feelings, and each time this is done with intention reinforced by desire more and more life is infused into the vision. Ignatius Loyola based his wonderful magical system of training on this fact.

Again, never build your visions if you are bored with them lest you undermine their vitality. Instead visualize another totally different but familiar symbol as a mental drill for a disobedient mind. Drill your mind during periods of 'dryness' with the visualization of the Tree of Life and vibrate gently its God-names. They are a potent cure for what some call 'the Dark Night of the Soul'.

It is a great help when building symbols in vision to feel that behind one is the life power of the Unmanifest waiting for any opportunity to find expression through forms that are created by a visualising imagination. Feel strongly that you have behind you andflowing through you the limitless energy and everlasting harmony of the Great Mother of All. Then by working AS IF this were so, one's natural abilities are transcended.

In working a moon ritual in group meditation, there are certain phenomena that practical work has brought to notice. Among these is the important fact that better results are to be got by working as a trinity. For example, the Hierophant if a man, will find that his powers are immensely enhanced if he will think out the implications of the following facts.

The Roman Church uses three priests for its High-mass. In the Vignettes of the 'Pert em Hru', i.e. 'Coming into the day', Osiris as the

Hierophant is supported by Isis and Nephthys. Hecate Triformis is a combination of Aphrodite-Selene-Hecate and represents the Powers of Heaven, Earth and the Inner World. Sinn, the Babylonian Moon God, was also Triune in his inner nature. In the Islamic faith, the Three Daughters of Allah retain the ancient names of the three aspects of the Arabian Moon Goddess. They are Al-Ilat; Al-Uzzaz; and Manat. Again the three Celtic Bridgets are three aspects of the great Celtic Moon Mother Anu, and so on.

There is much to be learned concerning the use that was made by the ancient initiated priesthoods of the fact that the gods and goddesses in the sphere of Yesod are three-aspected by watching with the inner eye what is done in group meditations by those Orders that have recovered something of these ancient methods from their own unpublished manuscripts as well as from the published works of Briffault and Frazer, and from Hastings' 'Encyclopaedia of Religion and Ethics'.

EXERCISE III.

At the pillars of Aurd-na-Rae: the High Place of the Moon.

In the place of Caoilte in a faint haze of golden light stood a smiling woman of the Sidhe very soft and young and graceful, and the man wondered if this were Niamh of the Golden Hair. But seeing his perplexity at this sudden change of guide the woman laughed and said, 'I am old, very old as you men count years, and yet I am ever-young, for unlike Eve I made not for myself a coat of skin. Your former partner Eve is now renewing her youth in TIR-FA-THONN, the land beneath the waters. And now that you have passed safely over An-na-Rea by the Bridge of the Moon I will take you the long green way over the wide spaces to Aurd-na-Rea. There between the Pillars of the Whispered Truth you may learn of the Great Mother; for it is She whom we also serve who are of the Dedannans, the children of Dana. But first look once again in this deep brown pool of An-na-Rea and tell me what you see'.

He gazed into the still dark water that now, seen from the West, reflected the trees of the fairy wood and the steep dark mountain beyond it. A faint mist rose and then cleared, and in the pool was a seemingly drowned land. A land of high towers, lofty trees, and bright colours where dwelt a people ever young, every happy, ever advancing in a wisdom that is not the result of human experience and suffering.

This is the land that some call the Summer land of the Astral Plane. Long ago it was called the Garden of Eden and Adam dwelt there with Lilith for his first wife. But because progress is slow in perfect happiness Adam was filled with a divine discontent. And so, when in deep sleep, he dreamed of Eve as the imperfection that should complete his own perfection. And when his dream exteriorized through intense desire he sought with her the golden wisdom that the sacred green all-wise snake would give him through failure. And so the two wandered from that golden land 'on the verge of the azure sea'. For Adam was divorced from his first inner and subjective love when he sought for the objective as Eve.

Lilith remained in Tir-fa-Thonn, the bright land that is in the Astral Sea, until the Moon Mother who rules the rise and fall of Astral tides called her to her temple that is within Aurd-na-Rea, the High-place of the Moon. There it can still be seen, it is said, as Hy Brasil: as long ago it was seen by Maildun - the Irish Seer, who saw it without the sight of his physical eyes by means of the two-petalled Lotus that is between them.

The vision vanished and the woman of the Aes-Shee moved up the green way through the heather, purple with its summer blossom and smelling like new honey, past golden furze bushes bright with yellow blooms. There was no sun nor were stars visible. Yet all details could be clearly seen in the green and faintly orange lights that cast the purple shadows of the sphere of Yesod where rules the Lord of the Moon who is the king of this Land of Life. He who is the first-born of the Great Mother Dana, the ruler of the non-human peoples of the Etheric and Astral planes of consciousness.

They stood before two great pillars. Beyond these pillars only faintly to be seen was a temple, and before it a throne - that of the Great Moon Mother who sat thereon.

The man stood alone before the Pillars of the Whispered Truth for his guide the Bean Sidhe [banshee] had vanished; and he sought to pass between them, but could not. Then he saw the sword of Life that flames red as blood between the Pillars of Life and Death, the Jachin and Boaz of the Temple of Solomon. He heard the right-hand pillar whisper - 'Moy Mell is barred to you without Eve'. The left pillar whispered also, 'Moy Mell is barred to you without Lilith'.

And then the blood-red sword whispered, 'If you would pass while living, here is the Key of the Door that is barred by me, for I am the Sword of Azrael. Come again as Adam bringing your Eve and your Lilith'.

The functional nature of the unit for leaving the Astral Garden is dual, for returning however it is Triune.

THE WATCHER AND THE TRIUNE DIVINITIES

In the Old Religion a snake symbolizes the inner wisdom that is intuition. Also in vision it is a symbol for a Lord of the Moon sphere. Cernunnos is often shown with serpents as is Hermes, and so are other wisdom gods.

Eve is the Moon. She is Woman as the man of the Earth-sphere knows her. Lilith is Woman as the Lords of the Moon-sphere know her. The Moon-sphere is positive and the Earth-sphere is negative, and both are contained within the etheric of that purposive entity which is called the Great Earth Mother, or the Great World Mother. She is a macrocosm and the human entity is a microcosm. The latter is also bi-polar. And the four poles of these two entities - the World Mother and the human being – can be linked so that the more potent will charge with life energy the less potent. The process by which the
microcosm consciously charges itself from its immediate macrocosmic superior is the so-called 'Yoga of the West'. It is the wisdom of the serpent according to the non-Semitic religions of pre-Christian times.

This Yogic process can be carried out by a single person working alone in meditation. It can also be carried out by two or three persons of opposite sexes in what may conveniently be called a ritual meditation. The most powerful training unit is either a man and two women, or a woman and two men. That is, Osiris supported by Isis and Nephthys, Adam with Eve and Lilith, or Isis supported by Osiris and Set, and Isis supported by Horus and Anubis.

A glance at the vignettes of the 'Pert-em-hru', or a study of the wall-paintings in the tombs and temples of Ancient Egypt will show how the ancient priest or priestess invoked divine energy into a Temple Ritual. For the Romans, Janus, who like the Qabalistic angel Azrael, sat at the Gates of the Inner World, is the personified guardian of this knowledge. And here it must be pointed out that knowledge (in such matters) is not the same thing as a belief, theory or speculation. Any one can speculate and theorize about the ancient teaching that is shadowed forth above, but something more than this is necessary in order consciously to pass the blood-red sword of the Angel of Death that guards the ever-open gate that is between the Pillars of the Here and the Yonder. But unlike the gates of the Roman temple of Janus Bifrons [two-headed] this gate is never closed (except to the living by the blood-red sword) for there is never peace between those twin brothers that are Life and Death, Osiris and Set, Vishnu and Shiva.

'On the day the Silver Cord is snapped and the Golden Lamp drops broken', you will, as it were in sleep, pass the sword of Azrael and the gates of Janus Bifrons, and you will then find that they are each of them the kindly helper who gives sleep to his beloved. But it is quite another matter to face the flaming sword that keeps the way through the Gate of Life and of Death (for they are not two things but one thing viewed from two aspects) and to consciously bring back to this earth tidings of that which in human language is said to be behind or beyond or within this ever-opened, yet closely guarded gate.

This conscious entry and return through the Gates of the West is the result of knowledge that can be gained by using this so-called Yoga of the West; however, the method itself can only be learned through the trial and error of practical experience.

In a certain sense Osiris on his bier is the candidate. But in another sense he is the officiating priest. Both have to take the way between the Western portals of night and day. Look closely at this scene, for Lilith, who is the Egyptian Nephthys, must come to the aid of Eve, who is Isis, the mysterious Sister, Mother, Wife of Osiris who may be either the candidate or the officiant at the double altar.

In certain of the mystery rituals Osiris is referred to as the child of two Mothers and the clue to this curious aphorism is to be found when and where the functioning priestly unit is triune. In the Old Religion the priest who stands at the altar as mediator between the Great World Mother and her devotees is also in his inner aspect a child of the two moon mothers. For he is the focussing-point for the consciously directed powers of Nephthys and Isis as energising negative and positive cosmic factors. Hints with regard to this point are given in the following quotations from the Litany of Nes-Amsu:

> Behold the lord Osiris… Are not the two impersonators of the goddess, and Hunnu,* the beautiful, approaching to thy shrine at this
> moment?
> Lo! the Bull,* begotten of the two cows Isis and Nephthys!
> He, the progeny of the two cows Isis and Nephthys, the child surpassingly beautiful!
> He appeareth unto us in thy image, like the one beloved.
> Behold! He [Osiris]* comethl '
> > Quoted from Wisdom of the East - 'The Burden of Isis',
> > The Litany of Nes-Amsu.

The proof of a pudding is said to be in the eating of it. It is equally true that the proof of the magical efficiency of a unit in any ritual technique is in the working thereof. The priest with the mask of Osiris had at his left shoulder a priestess wearing as her headdress the throne of Isis. At his right was another wearing the cup of Nephthys. In other ceremonies Isis functions with Horus and Set as her supporters. In modern psychological terms, reason (Osiris) is the focal point for the powers of superconsciousness and subconsciousness. In ancient times space was conceived of as having Osiris for the horizon line which forever hides Isis. Osiris is the ever-moving present that divides Isis, as the past, from Nephthys, the dark and ever-hidden future.

Religious psychology has taught that a man has within his soul his Isis and his Nephthys; Adam carries in his bosom both Eve and Lilith. A woman, as the microcosm of the macrocosmic woman, the Moon, has within her soul Osiris and Set, those great and vastly ancient gods that are the twin sovereigns of the moon phases. 'Hell,' it is said, 'knows no fury like a woman scorned,' a saying easy to understand when Set as the Red Lord of the dark moon phases becomes the ruler of a woman's inner emotional life - for is not Set the slayer of Osiris?

Analytical psychology tells much about these secret moon aspects of the soul, but the habitual working of magical rituals not only tells but also brings into manifestation much more than can the former method. Here is a list of triune divine manifestations that will repay study, provided the processes that have been described in the previous chapters have been brooded upon and used practically and with understanding in meditation.

(A) MALE
Shiva - Vishnu - Brahman
Set - Horus - Osiris (as Moon-Gods)
Ptah - Sokar - Ausar (as the primitive creative power and darkness, the Dweller in the Secret Place).
Ptah - Seker - Temu (the Lord of the Hidden Place).
Balor - Bress -Tethra (the three aspects of Buar-Ainech who is Cernunnos as the wearer of the Homed Moon).

(B) FEMALE
Hathor - Nephthys - The Green Isis (Aspects of Isis).
The Three Bridgets as aspects of Dana.
The Three Bridgets (Bride) as aspects of Anu.
Aphrodite - Persephone - Hecate.

(C) COMBINED
Ptah - Nefer-Tem - Sekhet (Sekhmet)
Horus - Set - Isis
Sinn - Merodach - Ningala
Nannar - Bel-enlil - Ishtar
Tammuz - Belit-Sheri - Ishtar
Tammuz - (Eresh-Ki-gal) - Ishtar (Allatu)
Osiris - Isis - Nephthys
Shiva - Kali - Durga
Adam - Eve - Lilith

The Master Jesus had a friendship with Martha and Mary, and you will not waste your time if you meditate upon the story of Jesus and the two Marys at the foot of his cross. One Mary is the Virgin, one is the Harlot, and the cross of Jesus is symbolic of the unfolded Black Altar of the Universe upon which the Divine Manifestor and Architect of the Universe is always being sacrificed in an unceasing ever-becoming. 'Je change sans cesse' is as true of the mind of the cosmos as it is of the mind of man.

Again ponder on the fact that the first human being the Christian conqueror of Death meets at his resurrection is Mary the Harlot, a very significant point for those who understand that Yesod is the Power House of both the universes - the Macrocosmic and the Microcosmic. Why also did Jesus call Mary and Martha to him when he went to the timb of Lazarus to perform a magical feat upon the dead?

These trinities have nothing to do with the father-mother-child combinations so delightfully explained by some students of comparative religion and folk-lore. There are divine forms for use in magical rituals. They are still potent and can be unpleasant and dangerous if used unskillfully by those who fail to balance Wisdom and Power in Harmony.

As a method of training the mind to realize through visualised symbols these ideas, draw a large red triangle on a sheet of paper. Put Harmony at the apex, Wisdom at the left basal angle, and Power at the right basal angle.

Draw a blue triangle with its apex downwards and label it in the same way. Let the red triangle be considered as Tiphareth, Netzach and Hod and the blue triangle as Netzach, Hod and Yesod. Remember however that these two triangles are in different states of consciousness, or on different planes of being. Or again, consider the red triangle to be Fire (not physical but metaphysical fire), and the blue triangle to be Water (also not physical). Now the qualities named at the angles refer not only to cosmic manifestations of the divine Henads or gods, but also to analogous psychological factors in the Soul of Man.

Use the red triangle for the negative feminine goddesses. Then draw with its apex upwards a third triangle in green, the fairy color, the sacred colour of those who work the moon magic in what the Celtic world calls Tir-nan-og. It too is in yet another dimension as you will soon discover when successful practical work begins.

Use this green triangle as follows. If you have a trinity of two gods and a goddess, place the goddess at the apex. If two goddesses and a male god, then place him at the apex. In a ceremony at the altar this rule is observed by those that wear the priestly masks. Visualize the apex of each triangle as touching the altar, and watch your reactions to this picture when it is firmly built in the astral temple.

Again, in magic the woman is the equal of the man. In the Mysteries of Eleusis the Hierophantissa played a part equal to that of the Hierophant; one of the former was able to boast that she had initiated no less than three Roman Emperors. In the highest of the three grades that the Mystae ordinarily achieved, the roles of the Hierophant and the Hierophantissa were equal even as late as in the Christian era. So picture yourself in the role of your sex, and behind you the two who serve at the altar with you.

Every woman has her right to face across the black altar the Divine Being that she and her assistants impersonate. Sometimes the old memories return at such a moment very clearly; so visualize carefully and feel deeply. Sit down in meditation, and as soon as the mind is quiet, visualise any temple sanctuary that appeals to you. In the centre is a black stone altar, a double cube about four and a half feet high. On it is the Sacred Light. You as priest or priestess stand at the altar facing east. Before you, dimly seen in the darkness of the sanctuary in the East, are the conventional forms of the three gods, or goddesses, or the mixed trinity you decide to use. Behind you are the two priests or two priestesses of the gods or goddesses that form the basal angles of the triangle.

Build that scene until it appears automatically the moment you are seated for your meditation. Now - as the *Watcher* - see what happens when the priestly figure that is you (as the Hierophant) invokes. When the meditation is finished record the results (if any) and your emotional results (if any).

You may get a surprise the first time you try this method. But in all probability (as happened to the author) you will get nothing without many weeks of steady concentrated visualizing with strong desire. So do not be discouraged - you value most that for which you have had to work hard.

133

Exercise IV.

THE HOSTING OF THE SIDHE

A) As a part of this Exercise, and before continuing the vision of Tir-nan-og, visualize clearly with strong feeling this glorious piece of English rhyming verse.

CHORUS

Some Maidens

Will they ever came to me, ever again,
    The long long dances,
On through the dark till the dim stars wane?
Shall I feel the dew on my throat, and the stream
Of wind in my hair? Shall our white feet gleam
    In the dim expanses?
Oh, feet of a fawn to the green wood fled,
    Alone in the grass and the loveliness;
Leap of the hunted, no more in dread,
    Beyond the snares and the deadly press;
Yet a voice still in the distance sounds,
A voice and a fear and a haste of hounds;
O wildly labouring, fiercely fleet,
    Onward yet by river and glen...
Is it a joy or terror, ye storm-swift feet?...
    To the dear lone lands untroubled of men,
Where no voice sounds, and amid the shadowy green
The little things of the woodland live unseen.
        Euripides, 'The Bacchae', translation by Gilbert Murray.

(B) *The Bean Sidhe (banshee) - fairy woman – led him back from the pillars to a spur of the heath lands, and they looked not back until she came to a low mound surrounded by silver-barked birch trees whose thick gnarled and twisted trunks showed their age. Handing him the branch with the silver blossom, she ordered him to touch the root and trunk of the largest birch which was in the centre of the path. As he did so the tree vanished and in its place was a temple-like portal across which was hung a heavy dark green curtain through which she entered and he followed.*

They were inside and in the transparent brown earth; a great mountain stretched below them and they started to descend its rough, rock-strewn

134

slopes by going further down into the deep. Swiftly they moved downwards in order to reach the top of the mountain upon which a brilliant city of gold and green appeared.

This world was indeed solid just as is that which is upon the surface of the earth, but one seemed to see the inside as well as the outside and the inside was outside the boundaries of the outside. One felt rather like Alice when through the looking-glass.

This city had walls of a semi-transparent green and gold, and it was made of stones that looked like a piece of glass that has been a long time on the sea-shore and has been marked by the grinding action of the stones and shells.

At the gate of the city were guards. Each was armed with a golden-headed spear and a round shield. They saluted the silver-like branch and allowed the Bean Sidhe and her companion to pass into a wide street which led to a tree-bordered square on the far side of which was a portal leading into a great palace, where a Prince of the fairy people met them.

'Your companion,' he said, 'had the right of entry, but you have to be vouched for by a guide. By what authority do you come?'

The Bean Sidhe showed the silver-white branch of blossom, the symbol that in the ancient Celtic Mysteries admits the would-be initiate in to the land that lies between the Here and the Yonder, and between the past and the present. It is the dimension that is between the outside and the inside, where consciousness is able to transcend the ever-passing present. Here the initiand, like Mohammed's coffin, seems to hang between heaven and earth. This is the Land of the Ever Young, because having no present there is no past and no future.

Time as generally understood by man, is not, for with the Sidhe time is but a graduated scale for the measuring of joy. There is no sorrow, no suffering, only degrees of joy and degrees of beauty, and degrees of wisdom; here, however, wisdom is not just being well-informed.

Yet they lack one thing which mankind has - suffering, and the joy that suffering ultimately brings. They live in an unending perfection, and because they are perfect, though in a way that man cannot even faintly comprehend, they can only remain in that state of perfection in which the great World Mother has placed them as they are the children of but one of her many forms of evolution. Men are mortal because Adam took Eve with him when he left the Garden of Eden, which is fairyland, to seek mortality as an escape from the timeless, spaceless perfection of Tir~nan-og.

'Now that you will be shown Tir-na-mbeo - the Land of the Ever Youthful - will you have me as your guide, or do you prefer to have this woman?' the Fairy Prince asked his visitor.

There was something in the way that both looked upon him that made the man realise that much hung upon that apparently simple and courteously put question. He read in both their eyes something that was almost like anxiety, an anxiety to escape from perfection it seemed, and he felt an unspoken appeal from the dark fairy woman beside him.

He asked that she might remain with him, and with a sigh the Fairy Prince left him, and the fairy woman took him into a garden immense as a park.

She sat beside him holding his right hand in her left; then she passed her right hand over his eyes and told him to watch the trees and flowers and to try to see how they manifested on the physical plane their real life which is the fairy world of the Moon-plane which some call the Astro-etheric.

The scenery had become just that of an ordinary earthly landscape in a rich, cultured man's private park. The fairy woman had grown dim to his sight, he no longer saw her form though he felt the energy pouring from her to him and he heard her anxious whisper 'Concentrate or I am lost for you'.

It was difficult to concentrate. Sight had grown abnormal; nothing was clear, and the wide landscape was dissolving in a seeming chaos of colour that lost itself in a mother-of-pearl-tinted haze. Only one form held - a beech tree, and in despair he compelled himself to see it as he knew it ought to be. A brief struggle, and then the tree and the park came once more into focus as a clear and beautiful astral garden.

'Now try to see the tree as a purposive intelligent entity,' he was told, and he felt a hand placed on the nape of his neck.

As he watched, the green of the beech-leaves and the faint silver colour of the bole seemed to merge in a form that was not the tree, and yet it was like the tree. He was no longer seeing the tree with his eyes - he was feeling it.

He was once again in his inner, subtler, Moon-body, and with it he saw and felt the Moon-body of the tree. Then appeared the tree spirit, the Deva, the Shining One who lives through the trunk and branches and leaves of the beech tree as a man lives through his torso, limbs and hair. That beech was very friendly and Moon-body to Moon-body they met, and as his Moon-body merged into that of the Lady of the Beech Tree the sensation of the nature of the seasons, of the caress of the sunlight, of the *stimulation of the bright increase of the waxing moon, and of the sleep-time that comes with the decrease of the waning moon were his.*

'You can merge thus into all life,' he was told; and then he saw; as the fairy sees, the flowers, the waterfalls, the rivers, and the brightly coloured holy mountain of Derrybawn, which means the home of the Shining Ones. He merged himself into the roaring life that was at the summit of that great and sacred mountain - and in so doing he took the initiation of the Lady of NATURE – the Green Isis - in her temple on the heather-clad hill-top that is above the deep ravine.

The fairy woman stood beside him on a small platform that overhung an immense gorge the bottom of which was almost lost in mists that rose from a dark, still lake. She stretched her arms as if to dive and whispered, 'I dare you!' and was gone.

Next moment both were speeding on the wings of thought downwards, and out from the blue mists below came the galloping Host riding from Knock-na-Rea. A pair of riderless horses sped beneath them like a flash. She took a gray horse and he a black mare. And hand in hand, with the flanks of the screaming gray stallion and the whinnying black mare touching, they raced across starlit astral space in the wake of the 'Hosting of the Sidhe'.

RETROSPECT AND SUMMARY
The Song of Diana (The Goddess of the Old Religion in Italy.)

'Endamone, Endamone, Endamone!
By the love I feel, which I
Shall ever feel until I die,
Three crosses on thy bed I make
And then three wild horse-chestnuts take;
In that bed the nuts I hide,
And then the window open wide,
That the full moon may cast her light
Upon a love so fair and bright,
And so I pray to her above,
To give wild rapture to our love,
And cast her fire in either heart,
Which wildly loves to never part:
And one more thing I beg of Thee!
If anyone enamoured be,
And in my aid his love hath placed,
Unto his call I'll come in haste.'

Quoted from 'Aradia' by Leland.

At the 'Twin' doors of the objective Divine Unconscious (as is said to have been the case at the dual-doored Crypt of Ancient Eleusis), stand three vast figures. On the left is that of the Great Queen, the Soul of the World, who is personified as the All-Mother Saraswati, Aima, Ama, Gè, Demeter, the Heavenly Isis - the Celestial Light and Source of Life, Great Diana, and Ishtar.

On the right is a youthful Queen with the 'Narcissus' on her brow, the young, and ever-virgin bride on the throne of the Under-World, ruler of the kingdoms of sleep and of dreams, She who is Death, and as such is also the 'Holder of the Secret of Life'. Kore, Nephthys, Belit-Sheri, Aradia the daughter of Diana, are but some of her personifications.

Between these two doors and in the centre is the 'Lord of the Ivy Crown' holding a winged thyrsus interlaced with two serpents. He is personified as Dionysos who is Life, Death and Resurrection, and as Osiris, the Risen Lord of Death.

It is wise today, as it was in the past, having passed and re-passed this dual-doored gateway, to place finger upon lip, for talking about psychic experiences, except to the teacher, breaks their magical validity. The initiated occultist, that is, he who has stood on the floor of the cave that symbolizes the Beyond, is usually chiefly interested in three things...

First is the training of his earthly personality, both body and mind, so that it shall become as sound an instrument for the work he has to do as he is capable of producing within the limitations of his Karma.

Then he spends much time and thought in meditation or in a potent type of ritual by means of which he, voyaging into other states of consciousness, endeavours to get into contact with the beings of other evolutions that are progressing along cosmic paths which are, so to speak, parallel to that taken by humanity.

And thirdly he aims at gaining conscious contact with entities that, being more evolved than himself, have for their sphere of operation realms of existence that are supra-physical. The occultist's early studies lie in the sphere of Yesod, which is that of the Machinery of this Universe as cosmic energy in action. In the past the initiated called these great beings, the Gods, and the Buddhists and Hindus today call them the Devas.

These three objectives were, and are, often pursued more or less simultaneously, though it is, as a rule, wiser to make some considerable progress with the first objective before the second and third are undertaken. All three methods seek to teach one how to live in the Universal Soul consciously.

Thus three levels of the mind are dealt with in the course of training: the conscious level, the unconscious level that is personal to each individual, and that still deeper and more primitive unconscious level that is common to all humanity and to all entities that are part of the evolving life of the Great Mother Isis, Ishtar, and Dark Diana of the many breasts.

The more materially-minded moderns think that man is the highest of God's creative acts. But in this matter they flatter themselves. In this physical world the human line of evolution may be higher than that of the pig, goat, bird or fish, but occultism is not concerned with the lines of evolution that have externalised completely into physical manifestation.

In this paper only the beings that belong to the Sphere of Yesod have been touched upon, and no attempt has been made to develop in the reader the contacts that give access to certain of the Great Devas that rule in Spheres of evolution that are other than human. Nevertheless some readers who are far advanced may have successfully touched certain of these great Beings that in the New Testament are called Powers, Principalities, Rulers, Elements or first principles. This leads up to the great truth that in the Mystery schools the teacher is not so important as the personality of his pupil - for all development must be self-development.

Masefield has written in one of his poems:

> Fate, that is given to all men partly shaped,
> Is ours to alter daily till we die.

And he has here put into modern English one of the famous and secret maxims common to the Mystery training processes of all times. This word 'secret', however, is used here in a very particularised sense. One great Master has talked of it as seed growing in secret, the grain growing secretly in the dark black earth. Here reference is made to what a certain type of teacher calls a Seed though: which is what this maxim is.

A Seed thought means that if you put with strong intention a magical idea into your visualizing imagination and build it clearly, and then with intention consign it to the fructifying darkness. of your unconscious mind, it will begin to grow in energy. If you go on repeating this process with strong intention every day even for but a few short moments when rising from and also when going to bed, this magical idea will in time come to energize your life and your expression of life in matter.

139

Suppose you feel drawn to the Old Religion, to the Mysteries of Diana in the sphere of Yesod. If your circumstances bar you from participating in them, and if you are unable to change those circumstances in the ordinary way, there is no need for you to sit down and do nothing. By working upon your unconscious mind you can change the *NATURE* of your relationship to your environment - a thing that Omar Khayyarn has hinted at and Aradia taught in the 'Song of Diana' just quoted.

Build the Green Ray pictures that have been given you. Strive to feel within yourself the joy that they are intended to produce in your emotional nature. If you can work yourself up into ecstasy - that is, to a state of consciousness that enables you to stand without yourself - a few moments are all that are necessary - in time you will so change that circumstances will cease to hinder, for you will have changed their relationship to yourself.

When the students is ready the Masters will come: for usually the they are more anxious to find us than we are to seek them. The first step is always preparation, and on its thoroughness depends the speed at which you will advance. So begin upon your own inner self - your first and last task in the Mysteries.

The Ancients used the Fire of the Wise to burn away the dross in their own personalities. The Fire of the Wise is the visualising imagination, As a man thinks in his heart, so is he. The modern rendering of that term 'heart' is subconscious mind. And the psychological rendering of this saying should be - As a man's subconscious mind sees him to be, so he is. The subconscious mind is not the reasoning mind. It is something far more primitive and powerful which works in picture-images and not in words. Its guide is feeling, not reason. In it are hidden the memories of the past aeons. In it are hidden the memories of the past aeons. In it also lie the potentialities that will determine the future for the cosmic subconscious mind that is Aradia, the ever-virgin daughter of the Dark Diana, the Cosmic Mother of the OLD RELIGION.

IN the imagery that has been given you here is hidden a method for doing two very different things: first for developing and maintaining and emotional drive that will enable you to get started on your task of 'finding the hidden Wisdom that contains all the ancient wisdoms of the World,' as one ancient worthy has declared; and secondly the construction of a FORM which will enable you to link your varying states of consciousness to their appropriate type of subtle matter in the Soul of the Great Mother.

When this form is adequately functioning, and when it is filled with the appropriate type of energy, you have within yourself an *ENS REALISSIMUM* which is as the Philosopher's Stone. It is a magical personality and it is the key to symbolism used when worshipping great Diana, the Compassionate Mother.

So long as you remember and act upon the ancient proverb, 'The Gods give their rewards only to those who sweat for them' you have, by virtue of this key, the power to function as a member of the priesthood of THE OLD RELIGION.

i William Wordsworth, *The Prelude.* Book 12. 208-218 (1850 edition)

ii http://www.isleofraasay.com/index.php/2016/11/06/the-water-horses-of-loch-na-mna/

iii https://en.wikipedia.org/wiki/Star_jelly_cite_note-timesonline-5

iv https://www.raasay.com/images/Newsletters/10%20Am%20Bratach%20Raasay's%20Community%20Newsletter%20September%202016.pdf

v *The Forgotten Mage*, p 29. Edited by Dolores Ashcroft-Nowicki, Aquarian Press 1986

vi Ibid

vii Phil Mason, *One in the Eye for Harold – Why everything you thought you knew about history is wrong.* Robson Press 2011

viii http://www.thymeraven.uk/

ix https://www.youtube.com/watch?v=61OOq60hISU

x http://hpb.narod.ru/EvocationApolloniusEL.html

xi *The Seventh Sense*, p253, Lyn Buchanan, Paraview 2003.

xii *The Western Mystery Tradition*, p57, Christine Hartley. Aquarian Press

xiii *Far Memory*, Joan Grant, Arthur Barker 1956

xiv http://www.fanad.net/lacus00.pdf

xv Report in the Sunday Times 14 November 1999

xvi *Celtic Christianity*, p31, Anthony Duncan, Element Books 1992

xvii See *Searching for Sulis*, Alan Richardson KDP 2019

xviii https://www.faena.com/aleph/articles/notes-on-the-symbolism-of-deer/

xix *Sea Room*, Adam Nicholson, Harper Collins 2013

xx Anyone who imagines that the Vatican has reformed, or that John Paul II and Pope Benedict XVI were almost saintlike, should read the very recent *In the Closet of the Vatican* by Frederic Martel

Printed in Great Britain
by Amazon

36394129R00085